About the

Dr. Arthur Mitchell, Professor of ⎯⎯⎯⎯ ⎯⎯y of
South Carolina, has written on a ⎯⎯⎯ ⎯⎯dern Irish and
Irish-American subjects. A native of ⎯oston, Massachusetts, he
was educated at Boston College, Boston University and Trinity
College, Dublin. Among his works are *Labour in Irish Politics,
1890–1930*; *Ireland, Irishmen and the American War of
Independence*; *History of the Hibernian Society of Charleston,
South Carolina*; (co-editor with Padraig O Snoddaigh) *Irish
Political Documents, 1870–1916, 1916–1922*; and *Revolutionary
Government in Ireland: Dáil Éireann, 1919–1922* (forthcoming).
He currently is writing a history of the rise of the Boston Irish
to political power in the 1880s.

JFK and His Irish Heritage

JFK
and His
Irish Heritage

ARTHUR MITCHELL

Moytura Press

Do na O'Mistéil
agus na O'Gallchobhair

This book was designed and typeset by
Seton Music Graphics, Ltd., Bantry, Co. Cork for
Moytura Press, 4 Arran Quay, Dublin 7

© 1993 Arthur Mitchell

A catalogue record for this book
is available from the British Library

ISBN 1-871305-19-5

Printed in Ireland by
Betaprint, Ltd, Dublin

CONTENTS

INTRODUCTION

Walking out of the Irish Parliament building with Kenneth O'Donnell in 1963, John F. Kennedy asked him whom he thought were the best politicians in America. O'Donnell replied: 'Mayor Richard Daley of Chicago and Senate Majority Leader Mike Mansfield.' Kennedy agreed, adding, 'The Irish do seem to have an art for government.' Then he stopped: 'Perhaps we are both prejudiced.' [1]

This is a study of John F. Kennedy and his sense of Irish identity and his relationship with Ireland. I hope it sheds some light on the role of ethnicity in American life during the period from the 1940s to the 1960s, and, as well, on the connection between the millions of Americans whose roots in the United States reach back but a few generations to their kith and kin in Europe.

I first encountered John Kennedy in 1952 during his campaign for the US Senate. Like about a million other people around Boston, my background was Irish Catholic, and my family had a strong interest in politics. I had heard stories about famous political battles and personalities, but I do not recollect anything about the Kennedys, particularly John F. Kennedy. One Sunday afternoon my mother, Alice Gallagher Mitchell, the politician in the family, asked me if I wanted to go with her to a Kennedy 'tea party' in our city of Quincy. In attendance were about three thousand women, three or four men and one boy, who stood at the back. Walking on to the stage was

a group of Kennedy women, led by Rose Kennedy, and a
young man on crutches. John Kennedy delivered a short,
essentially non-political talk about, I think, the New
England fishing industry. The Kennedys then proceeded
to greet and meet all the ladies present.

I was very struck by this person. He was different from
the other politicians I had seen or heard about in my
limited experience. He obviously came from a different
world than mine and everyone else that I knew. He was
well-spoken, reserved, understated, almost scholarly,
yet friendly and attractive. At least he looked like one of
our own. Because of my family background, I had a
pronounced ethno-centric view of politics and society.
Perhaps an unusual preoccupation, but there it was. I
recall a girlfriend calling me an 'Irish fanatic'! There is,
of course, a real danger in judging people on the basis of
their background.

Later, much later, I found out that various ethnic groups,
despite generations, suburbanisation, etc., retained distinctive values and attitudes. Moreover, people seemed
generally to know of their background or origins. A
sampling in the 1980 and 1990 US census if expanded to
the population as a whole would make those of Irish
self-identification the third (behind German and English)
largest group in the country representing about forty
million people (and for those of mixed ancestry, the
second). It seems to me that those values and attitudes,
inherited from our forebears, are the predominant factor in shaping the character and personality of the
United States.

At that time, I was very pleased that Kennedy was an
Irish Catholic Democrat. He seemed to me to be a model
of the person I would like to be. I cut out his picture
from his campaign leaflet, framed it and put it on my

bedroom wall, where it remained for long after he was elected President in 1960. I still have it.

I closely followed his Senate career and his rise to national prominence. I remember being at a back-room gathering (to which my friend Jim Watson and I had invited ourselves) at the 1956 Massachusetts Democratic state convention. Kennedy had just emerged victorious from a bruising battle for control of the party organisation. As I stood watching, he thanked a grizzled party veteran for his support. Hanging on to this man's arm was his daughter, who clung to her father in pride while she looked at Jack with awe and delight. What a handsome devil he was. My mother and my sister Helen, a young, good-looking nurse, went to meet Senator Kennedy in his Washington office. Kennedy warmly assured Helen that he would call on her services if needed, etc. Mom told me that she felt like the third person in a two-party conversation. Four years later my other sisters, Betty and Jane, lined up with their families along a fence at Hyannis airport to shake hands with the President of the United States. Happy memories.

During that time I became increasingly interested in his sense of self-identity. Would someone like Kennedy have the need for an ethnic awareness, or was that just something that the older school of politicians liked to trot out at election time? As far as I could figure out, at that time he was oblivious to this. I never heard of a statement by him either acknowledging his Irishness or any other ethnic consideration, but, I thought, this is not something that the new breed was concerned with or found politically advantageous. For several years I noted that he did not participate in the St. Patrick's Day parade in South Boston or any other Irish festivities held around 17 March in Boston, but he did appear in 1958, when

running for re-election, with Jackie at his side and a
Kelly green tie around his neck. Any politician would do
as much. Although he was smiling and waving as he
rode along, I recall that he didn't seem very comfortable
in this role.

It was not until 17 July 1960 when he returned to
Boston with the Democratic Presidential nomination in
hand that I saw him address this matter of roots. At the
airport he declared that when his great-grandparents
came from Ireland they brought with them only their
strong desire for freedom and opportunity. Now this, I
thought, is what I had been waiting for! It gave me a
great deal of pleasure to see 'one of our own' reach this
level of politics and, at the same time, acknowledge his
heritage. I also recognised that his position was politically
astute. Who could fault a candidate, even if he was a
Catholic or whatever, if he celebrated America as the
land where people from abroad earned the right to be
citizens and participants? I also knew that he needed the
overwhelming majority of the votes of people of 'newer
stock', many of whom had voted for the Republican
Eisenhower, if he was to be elected. Yet he also needed
to reach out to old stock Protestant voters and others.[2]

Although I did not know it then, Kennedy had a keen
sense of the significance of his quest. The historian
Theodore W. White has written about a night-time, cross-
country flight with him, in which Kennedy discussed
with understanding and sympathy the roles of various
ethnic groups, including their own — the Irish and the
Jews — in the American political spectrum. As White
noted, they were talking about ethnicity, something not
easy to pin down, but it is there if you chose to make it so.[3]

My political and personal identification with Kennedy
was nearly complete. I jumped up and down with

excitement and apprehension during his television debates with Nixon; his performance was flawless. On election eve, I stood on Boston's Washington Street to see him ride by and participated in an uproarious tribute. I recall it as a clan welcoming its conquering hero home. Despite the near hysteria of the crowd that night, Kennedy stood up in his convertible calmly, almost coolly, acknowledging this reception. Of course, he must have been close to total exhaustion and he had two more appearances yet to make, including a final national television address. The morning after the election, when he had finally been declared the winner, I shed a few tears, happy with the result but also thinking that this outcome washed away some of the pain experienced by millions of immigrants and their children at the hands of those hostile to the new-comers, and remembering my family talking about Governor Al Smith of New York, part Irish and Catholic, who had been defeated in his quest for the Democratic nomination in 1928. I suppose I was being histrionic, but that is the way I felt about it. Furthermore, I wanted to be an historian. My parents were getting up for work when I had the satisfaction of being the bearer of the good news: Kennedy won!

I recall a wave of happiness and pride sweeping across the Irish-Americans around my way. Others seemed to feel the same way. Lynell Carter, a black friend of mine at Boston University, told me that his family was overjoyed with the result. Jewish students that I knew were also extremely pleased. A few weeks later, when Lynell asked me to join in picketing Woolworths in Boston to get the company to end segregation in its southern stores, I told him, somewhat impatiently, that there was no need for this activity, as the new administration, my people, would see to all that. As time was to show, Lynell had the right approach.

Everything about the Kennedy Presidency was of intense interest to me. I was pleased that he surrounded himself with a group of Irish-American advisors and functionaries, the so-called 'Irish Mafia'. His anger and determination in facing down the attempt of the steel companies to raise prices in April 1962, after he had won the agreement of the unions for modest improvements in benefits, seemed to me to be a characteristically Irish response. There was also, of course, his cool and astute handling of the Cuban missile crisis. I cannot recall any bungling, inappropriate appointments, scandals or the like; the machinery of government seemed to be responsive and effective. His public style — intelligent, articulate, witty, idealistic — was a model for millions. Thus, I was impressed and proud of his performance as President. This assessment of his conduct of office was shared by a majority of Americans at the time of his death.[4]

One thing I did not like was the building of a family dynasty. When Ted Kennedy ran against Eddie McCormack for the Democratic Senate nomination in 1962, I voted for McCormack. Given the alignments in this political donnybrook, my voting for the 'other side' resulted in my mother calling me a traitor! (For that matter, for taking a stand against Johnson's Vietnam policy, I voted for Eugene McCarthy over Robert Kennedy in the 1968 Massachusetts presidential primary.)

Kennedy's presidential visit to Ireland in 1963 riveted my attention; I was planning to go there to study. I recall Kennedy paying tribute in Wexford to John Barry, 'father of the American navy', whose sword was in his White House office. One of my grandmothers, Annie McGowan of Galway town, told me when I was a little boy that we were related to Barry. Kennedy also praised the many Irishmen who had fought in the American Civil War. It occurred to me later that none of the Kennedys or Fitzgeralds had served in that conflict, while my great-grandfather, Patrick Gallagher from Galway, had done so and was at the battle of Gettysburg. Who did these Kennedys think they were? Then I discovered that one of my great-grandmothers was named Bridget Murphy, just as was one of Jack Kennedy's. A possible connection? Ah, but there were a lot of Bridget Murphys, and Patrick Murphys, in Ireland and Boston in those days.

The last time I saw Kennedy was in connection with the battle between Teddy Kennedy and Eddie McCormack. On a fine early September afternoon he flew up to Boston from Cape Cod to vote at his precinct on the back side of Beacon Hill. I have never seen a handsomer couple than Jackie and Jack that day. They both smiled to the crowd and the President walked across the street to shake hands with one older man he apparently knew. Perfect theatre! When I went to Ireland for graduate study in October 1963 I stepped into the backwash of the President's visit of four months before. So many people wanted to tell me about what a great event it had been. Then came 22 November. I observed that Kennedy's death was taken by the Irish people as a personal loss, as it was by me and others like me. I recall my mother saying to me a few years later, 'Nothing has gone right in this country since Kennedy died.'

Through the years my youthful interest in Irish people and their doings has persisted; my research and writing for thirty years has been in modern Irish and Irish-American history. Also, I have read all the Kennedy biographies, observed the family's various activities and told my students about the man I 'knew' who became President. I have remained most interested in this business of roots, ethnic awareness and Ireland. I have also noted that the biographies have had little to say about these matters, or not enough as far as I was concerned. Was it because they were really unimportant parts of his life, or was it because these were matters that had been overlooked by neglect or indifference? It was time for me to write about this, and the thirtieth anniversary of John F. Kennedy's presidential visit to Ireland provided the occasion.

The narrative of this work traces the migration from Ireland of the Fitzgeralds and Kennedys in the late 1840s to continuing Kennedy connections with Ireland through the early 1990s — almost a century and a half! There are also 24 documents dealing with John F. Kennedy. Documents sometimes can be lifeless and boring, but Jack Kennedy, at the height of his form, always had vitality, style and texture in his verbal and written communications.

In the text, for the sake of convenience, I generally have used the term Irish to refer to both the people of Ireland and those of Irish extraction in the United States. As natives of Eire are aware, there is a considerable difference between Irish-born people and Irish-Americans. Yet there is a real connection. In many ways those people who have chosen to retain, and even celebrate, their Irish background share many of the beliefs, viewpoints and values of the people of Ireland. Such was the case of John Fitzgerald Kennedy.

As you will observe, I occasionally have wandered from the main theme of this work as I wanted to briefly address other matters that to my mind are related to the subject at hand.

Go raibh maith agat / With many thanks

I am most grateful to the staffs of the National Library of Ireland, the Kennedy Library in Boston, particularly David Powers, Maura Porter, June Paige and Ronald Whealan, and Marvin Light and Sherrill Pinckney of the University of South Carolina Salkehatchie Library, Rick Ewig of the University of Wyoming Library and Peter Drummey of the Massachusetts Historical Society for their help in my research. My sincere thanks also to Sean Reidy of the Kennedy Centre in New Ross, County Wexford, Thomas P. O'Neill, retired lecturer at University College, Galway, Frank D'Arcy of Magee College, Derry, Padraig O Snoddaigh, Father Thomas Fagan, Joseph M. Griffin, as well as to Dan Ruff, Tye Johnson, Wayne Chilcotte, David Heisser and Stephanie Sanders of the University of South Carolina-Salkehatchie Campus, James M. Watson, John W. Downey, Francis Costello, John J. Duffy, Grainne Maire Mitchell, William E. Gerry, Tadgh Kennedy, Jonathan Leahy, Mairead Ni Chiosoig, Simon Bourke, Kevin O'Byrne and Sean O Luing. Gerard O'Connor and David Givens of Moytura Press, Dublin, have done excellent work in preparing the text for publication. I am also grateful to Vincent Doyle, editor of the *Irish Independent* for permission to include the articles by Frank D'Arcy and Frank O'Connor, to Donald Trelford, editor of *The Observer*, for allowing me to use the article by Patrick O'Donovan and to Edward S. Skillis, publisher of *Commonweal*, for permission to include the article by John Cogley. Once again Milton Harden generously has guided my way through the world of word processing. Lastly, my thanks to my wife, the former Marie O'Donoghue Leahy, for her assistance and encouragement.

It is often said that we cannot relive the past, but writing
this short work has greatly stimulated my recollections
of a memorable period, of Boston in the 1950s and
Dublin of the 1960s, a time of youth and hope, of progress
and achievement.

ARTHUR MITCHELL
University of South Carolina
September 1993

Chapter One

FAMILY AND POLITICS

John Fitzgerald Kennedy was the first, and to date ónly, Catholic to become president of the United States. He was also the first president who was clearly of original Irish stock. This is an inquiry into how he viewed his ethnic roots, how other people saw this and what, if any, significance this had on his life and times.

There had been several other presidents with Irish ancestry, but all of them were the descendants of immigrants from the northern province of Ulster, among the Protestant Scottish-descended part of its population. A notable example was Andrew Jackson, both of whose parents were born in Ireland. In fact, there have been three presidents (Jackson, James Buchanan and Chester Arthur) with a parent born in Ireland, more than in any other country. Andrew Johnson, whose mother was Mary McDonough and a Catholic, Ronald Reagan, with Tipperary forebears, and Bill Clinton, whose mother's maiden name was Cassidy, are the other presidents of original Irish stock, at least in part. But all of Kennedy's people were Irish.[1]

Even in the colonial period there had been substantial emigration from Ireland to America. People of Irish birth or descent were the third largest group in the 13 colonies, after the English and Africans.[2] Irish migration continued in a steady flow until the later 1840s, when it

became a mighty torrent of people. The political effects
of this tide could be seen in the late 1860s, with the rise
of the Fenians, a revolutionary nationalist movement. In
the 1880s Irish political organisations took over many of
the cities. There were Irish-born mayors in New York,
Boston and elsewhere. The Irish had established a political foundation. Given their preoccupation with politics
and government, there arose the hope and desire that
one of their own would one day make it to the top — to
the White House. With the resurgence of the Democratic
Party beginning in 1910, a permanent and growing bloc
of Irish-Americans were elected to the national House of
Representatives, with a few making it to the Senate.
Several Irish-Americans were elected governors. During
the struggle for Irish independence from 1916 to 1921, a
powerful campaign of support was formed in America,
which led many Irish people to assume that their
separated cousins were in positions of effective power.
President Eamon de Valera, who led the movement in
the US for a year and a half, found it necessary to deflate
this assumption. He told Dáil Éireann, the Irish national
assembly, in August 1921 that 'the Irish were very influ-
ential in Irish centres like Boston in local or municipal
politics, but they had no influence in national politics'.[3]

All during the 1920s much attention focused on the
quest of Governor Alfred E. Smith of New York and his
quest for the presidency. Although he was only part Irish
in background, Al was seen as the best of the Irish Catholic
big-city political culture. His overwhelming defeat as
Democratic nominee in 1928 was viewed by many people
as being due, at least partly, to his religion. Once again
the resurgence of the Democratic Party in the early 1930s
carried Irish-Americans into political office, this time in
unprecedented numbers. One of the beneficiaries of this

development was the Kennedy family, late of Boston. Irish political involvement did not abate. According to a recent study, those of Irish ancestry remain the most politically active group in the US. Another study shows that this group rose to be second only to Jews in terms of income and education.

John F. Kennedy's Irish connection goes back to his great-grandparents — Patrick Kennedy and Bridget Murphy, and Thomas Fitzgerald and Rosana Cox, all of whom were Famine-era immigrants. As was common in large Irish communities, all of their children married Irish-Americans. Both of Kennedy's grandfathers were professional politicians who rose from being ward bosses to become powerful political figures in Boston in the early years of this century.[4]

After their marriage, Kennedy's parents were detached from Irish groups and organisations in Boston and later in New York where they moved in 1926. They had had experience of Irish songs, meetings, political infighting and the rest since childhood. To them, the Irish connection and background was probably seen as a given condition; they were looking to a wider world. Joseph Kennedy was later to say that his boyhood home had been filled with talk about Ireland and Irish people, as well it should have been, given Patrick Kennedy's constituency! The son did have some feeling towards Ireland: when once asked why he disliked some English people, he replied that he could never forgive their government for setting loose the Black and Tans, a brutal paramilitary force, in an effort to stifle the movement for Irish independence. He also knew his own people in Boston. He once told Dave Powers (JFK's personal aide), that more Irish died of jealousy than of cancer. By the mid-1920s he found his abundant social and family ambitions blocked by

discrimination because of his religion and ethnic background; he said this is why he left Boston. Joe Kennedy
pursued money, power and a full life. Rose Fitzgerald
Kennedy supervised the raising of a brood of children,
travelled often on her own or with her sister and remained
devoted to her religion. Yet this family, in each generation,
maintained a connection with Ireland in the century and
more that separated them from there. Given their means,
access, political careers and ambitions, this is hardly
surprising.[5]

Patrick Kennedy was born in Dunganstown, County
Wexford in 1833. Two of his forebears had been in the
Rebellion of 1798. The third son of a tenant farmer, he
emigrated to Boston when he was twenty-five. There he
worked as a cooper on the East Boston docks, married
Bridget Murphy, another native of County Wexford, and
died of cholera at the age of thirty-five. His widow worked
in a variety of jobs to support the children. Their son, also
Patrick, after a career as a publican, legislator and businessman, travelled to Ireland in 1913 and met his relatives.
Letters were exchanged and his kin retained some
memory of this connection. He died when Kennedy was
twelve, so John would not have heard about much from
this grandfather, but his father often talked about the life
and times of Grandpa Kennedy. As the dominant
politician in an Irish community of East Boston, Pat was
supportive of a variety of Irish organisations. In the
period 1919–20, he bought a twenty-five dollar bond in
the fledgling Republic of Ireland, which, for a man of his
means, was a minimal gesture.[6]

John Kennedy's other grandfather, John F. Fitzgerald,
whose long political career included service as congressman and mayor, was the son of an immigrant from
Bruff, County Limerick; his wife's people also came from

Limerick — Lough Gurr. He first visited Ireland with his family, including daughter Rose, in 1908. At the end of his long life he declared that this visit was the highlight of all his travels. According to one report of a later visit, 'Honey Fitz' rushed around the countryside by car.[7] John Kennedy was later to say that his grandfather claimed a connection with the county of origin of any Irish person he met. As late as 1947 he told Jack that his Fitzgeralds came from Tipperary![8] Fitzgerald had a considerable interest in his Irish heritage and he was in a good position to transmit this to his grandchildren. His consuming interest, however, was in politics, Boston and Boston politics. Rose Kennedy later said that as a result of listening to the stories of his grandparents John was aware of the severe discrimination that the emigrant Irish and their children encountered.[9]

Joseph Patrick Kennedy

In his spectacular business career, Patrick's son Joe Kennedy surrounded himself with a coterie of Irish-American staffers (sometimes called henchmen); he could rely on their intelligence, loyalty and discretion — they could keep their mouths shut about Joe's various activities; his son John was to do the same. During the 1920s he amassed a fortune from stock market speculation, but had been rebuffed by Yankee Protestant high society in Boston. He was turned down for membership of a country club in Brookline, the Boston suburb in which he lived after his marriage. Another incident concerned a temporary, summer-time membership in an exclusive golf club; he later commented: 'Those narrow-minded bigoted sons of bitches barred me because I was an Irish Catholic and son of a barkeep. You can go to

Harvard and it doesn't mean a damned thing. The only thing these people understand is money.' Objection to the Kennedys was not simply because of their Irish Catholic identity, but also because of the way Joe Kennedy made money and the reputation of 'Honey Fitz' among Yankee Protestant Republicans. Shunned by the social leaders of this group, Kennedy moved his family to New York City in 1926. He later made the curious statement about what probably was the most Catholic city in America: Boston was 'no place to bring up Catholic children'.[10]

In the 1930s, due to his financial and personal backing of Franklin Roosevelt, the President appointed Kennedy to high office, culminating in 1938 with his appointment as Ambassador to Britain. Kennedy sometimes complained when newspaper reports labelled him as being Irish or Irish-American. He once declared: 'I was born here. My children were born here. What the hell do I have to do to be an American.' Privately these were the terms he applied to himself, a man of ethnic America, and to others like him. He told James Roosevelt, the President's son, 'I'm intrigued by the thought of being the first Irishman to be Ambassador from the US to the Court of St. James.' When Harold Ickes wondered why Kennedy wanted London, Tommy Corcoran supplied an answer: 'You don't understand the Irish. London has always been closed to him'; now the situation would be completely reversed. Franklin Roosevelt had several reasons for making this appointment. First, Kennedy wanted it. Moreover, Roosevelt had ancestral resentment towards the English and was offended by British imperiousness in official contacts. Sending over a lively, outspoken character of Irish Catholic background, Roosevelt declared, was 'a great joke, the greatest joke in the world'. He also wanted Kennedy out of the way and, anticipating war and Britain's need for US support, he probably recognised the value in having Kennedy in that position to defuse opposition from many Irish-Americans.[11]

It was in this position that Kennedy came in direct contact with Ireland. Although he had already taken his family on a couple of European tours, they had not included Ireland. When he arrived in London, the Irish and British Governments were in the process of negotiations concerning a variety of matters that were hangovers from the Anglo-Irish conflict of the early 1920s. Joe jumped into the middle of it.

Before the negotiations began, Eamon de Valera sent a special emissary, Frank Gallagher, to Washington to urge the US Government to give support to the Irish Government, asking him to 'use your influence to get the British Government to realise what would be gained by reconciliation and to get them to move whilst there is time. In a short while, if the present negotiations fail, relations will be worsened.'[12] Roosevelt responded by informing the Irish leader:

> I have taken the course of asking my good friend, Mr. Joseph P. Kennedy, who sails today for England to take up his post as Ambassador, to convey a personal message from me to the Prime Minister, and to tell the Prime Minister how happy I should be if reconciliation could be brought about. As an old friend I send you my warm regards.

De Valera was impressed by the Kennedy appointment, believing it would help the Irish position.[13]

Shortly after his arrival in London in April, Kennedy told British officials that Roosevelt had a 'keen' interest in seeing a fruitful outcome to the negotiations and American public opinion would respond positively to

concessions to Ireland.[14] Looking at the distinct likelihood
of war with Germany and the ultimate need for American
support, Neville Chamberlain's Government decided
conciliation was the best policy. In those circumstances
was it not better to have a friendly Ireland than a hostile
nation behind you? The result was the 1938 Anglo-Irish
agreement which cleared up the controversy over pay-
ments of Irish land annuities to the British Government
and transferred naval facilities to the Irish Government;
it did not address the matter of the partition of Ireland.
Kennedy was delighted with the agreement and received
praise for his assistance. He believed that de Valera was
mistaken to emphasise partition. Historians have doubted
that he had any real influence on it, but it would be untrue
to say that he was not involved in the process. De Valera,
for one, was grateful and, as Chancellor of the National
University of Ireland, offered him an honorary doctorate.[15]

Kennedy had been angling for an honorary degree
from Harvard, but this did not materialise. In London he
inquired about the possibility of such from Trinity College,
Dublin. At this point he decided to take up de Valera's
offer; after all, it was the first offer he had received from
anywhere. De Valera responded by declaring that 'everyone
who got to hear of it was overjoyed when they learned
Kennedy was coming to the land of his ancestors'.

Kennedy spent three days in Ireland, arriving by
chartered plane on 7 July accompanied by his eldest son
Joseph Jr., his friend and assistant Edward Moore and
journalist (and personal publicist) John B. Kennedy.
Rose Kennedy decided not to come due to bad flying
conditions. Another son, John F., was in England or
nearby in France at this time but did not make this trip.
Given his history of childhood sickness, he may well
have been ill.[16]

The Kennedy visit was the lead story in the Dublin daily press. At several functions and talking with reporters, Kennedy spoke of his Irish background. He declared that his sisters kept track of ancestors but they 'did not think he was likely to find relatives in Ireland now'. In any case, he said he was sorry that he would not have time to visit Wexford and Clonakilty 'where he thought he may have some family connections'. In fact his sister Loretta Connelly had sent to his New York office what information she had when Kennedy was nominated in February but he had not contacted her about the visit.[17] Some of the Kennedy relations in Wexford later said they had not realised they were connected to the Ambassador.[18] Throughout his life, he showed slight interest in his extended family beyond his two sisters and resident relatives: he had created his own large immediate family. Its members would be visiting Ireland, 'in installments, he declared with a smile', which they eventually did.[19]

He declined to talk about Irish unity and the ending of partition, but spoke freely on the Anglo-Irish agreement which he said was a 'step in the right direction'. At the ceremony conferring the degree, the ambassador was hailed by the Rev. Thomas Corcoran, a leading member of the faculty, as one 'who has wrought nobly as a pro-vider for his own great people and their welfare'. Kennedy declared he was so moved by being in Ireland he said that he was afraid to speak at a Dublin Castle banquet the next day because he might burst into tears of joyful homecoming. He did manage a few words, among which were: 'My parents and grandparents talked ever of Ireland, and from my youth I have been intent upon this pil-grimage.' He also spoke of reconciliation, first between America and Britain and then between Britain and Ireland: 'Between my country and Great Britain there have been two wars. Happily there is never to be another. Between this land of my fathers and the British there have been many wars. Happily there is never to be another.'

He never came back. He did, however, contribute something to Ireland and Irish people. In his own way, he used American power and influence to push negotiations for the 1938 treaty. Furthermore, as late as 1946 he was arguing the case for de Valera concerning post-war problems with the US Government in private correspondence with American officials. He provided a model of a person of clear Irish extraction who reached high levels in business and politics. In addition, of course, he founded a family that would have further to do with Ireland. When John F. Kennedy arrived in Ireland twenty-five years later as President of the United States he referred to Eamon de Valera as 'an old and valued friend of my father'.

As a result of his experiences in London, Joe did not become an Anglophile. He told Roosevelt: 'I hate all these god-damned Englishmen from Churchill on down.' According to one biographer, he remained the way he began: 'In taste, demeanor and even political orientation, a rather thoroughgoing Boston Irishman.'[20]

John Fitzgerald Francis Kennedy: Young Jack

Except for brief periods, the Kennedy boys did not attend Catholic schools and thus did not associate with children of their own religious and ethnic background. This was also true where they lived — in Brookline, Mass., Bronxville, N.Y. and at Hyannisport. Their education was almost entirely in the Yankee and Protestant mode of the private schools of New England. Yet with having Joe Kennedy for a father and Honey Fitz as a grandfather, they were aware of their Irish Catholic roots. Then there

was the influence of household employees, most
were Irish-born or Irish-Americans. Kathleen, JF1
got the nickname of Kick from one of these, '
Convoy. In his thesis on the Kennedy family, M
J. Rosanova declares: 'Most important for "meani
the definition of who we are" and "the sense in bein
— these indisputably ethnic servants exercised consi
able effect upon the household network.'

In her memoirs Rose Kennedy declared that Jac
'delighted in' his Irish heritage and heard stories 'abou
the miserable conditions under which the immigrants of
the 1840s and 50s had arrived in Boston, and the poverty
and social disdain they suffered there as "muckers" and
the like . . . .' As a happy go-lucky young man, he did not
appear to be concerned with this.

There was nothing vague about Kennedy's background — it was all Irish and Boston. All eight of his
great-grandparents were famine-era Irish immigrants;
his grandparents, aunts and uncles all married in the
Irish-American community of Boston. Although the
Kennedy boys were sent to private Yankee schools, the
writer Joe McCarthy noted that while at Harvard all of
them had as their best friend persons of Irish Catholic
background. They met them on the football team, but
football was not all of it.

At these schools Kennedy in fact encountered anti-
Catholic and anti-Irish feeling among some students. At
the Noble and Greenough junior school, he was aware
that his brother and himself 'were probably the first and
only ones who were Catholics, probably the only Irish
Catholic family'. Name-calling and fist fights ensued,
with brother Joe doing the fighting.

Kennedy once said that he failed to be admitted to
Groton, the top prep school, because of his Irish Catholic

identity. He had to suffer the ignominy of going to Choate. When the headmaster at that school denounced some students who were negligent in their studies and other responsibilities as 'muckers', Jack proceeded to organise a Muckers Club, as a result of which his father was called in and this act of defiance was quelled. Afterwards, Joe told his son that he was 'astonished' that Jack did not know that the word mucker had been a term of derision tossed at Irish labourers. He also wondered if Headmaster St. John was aware of this, but St. John probably was thinking in terms of English usage; private prep schools modelled themselves on the English 'public' schools. Yet a staff member later recalled that George St. John was prejudiced against Irish Catholic 'upstarts'.

At Harvard, due to his religion and his 'colourful' grandfather, he was not invited to join any of the top clubs until his Anglo-Protestant roommates declared that they would refuse all invitations while he was excluded. One of his classmates later said the objection was that Jack was 'such an obvious Boston-Irish type'. He failed in both attempts to win student office — for freshman class president and junior class student council.

Years later one of the Kennedy girls recalled that the Kennedy clan was not socially accepted in Hyannisport by the Republican Yankee residents of the resort. To some of these people the Kennedy home was known as the 'Irish house'. When walking through Louisburg Square in the heart of Boston's Beacon Hill an acquaintance noted the cobblestone street to which a Kennedy sister replied: 'Those aren't cobblestones, they're Irish heads.'[21]

The Kennedy older sons, Joe Jr. and Jack, as well as Kathleen, spent some time in London when their father was ambassador. The one that was most influenced by this experience was Kit, who married an Anglo-Irish nobleman and was in the process of doing it again when her young life came to an end. England did not seem to have left a mark on Joe Jr., but there are claims that it did on Jack. One of his English friends, Hugh Fraser, thought this was the case. David Nunnerley, who wrote a short book on Kennedy and Britain, makes him out to be an Anglophile, quoting an unnamed 'intimate friend' who declared Kennedy gradually outgrew the nasty 'anti-British elements' in him and 'by the end you couldn't have found a more British person'. He obviously admired the cool self-confidence of the upper-class young people he associated with, but, as will be seen, he could be a different person according to his company.[22]

Kennedy had a good knowledge of English literature, probably more than most liberal arts students. Several of his favourite books when he was a young man were by English authors. The nationality of the authors probably was not as important as was the fact that the books were about adventurous, dynamic people. Kennedy spent a total of just a few months in England. In 1935 he went there to study (at eighteen years of age) at the London School of Economics, but did not attend due to illness and returned home in less than a month. He was in England for a short period in the summer of 1938 and again in 1939 when he spent about six months travelling in a Europe on the eve of war.[23]

Jack Kennedy met a lot of young English people when he was there and he maintained contact with a few of them. One friend, David Ormsby-Gore, served as British ambassador when Kennedy was President. He liked British tailoring in men's clothings; many people do. Later he spent no more time in England than any other globe-trotter. Even as a young man he did not have a romantic view of the position of Britain in the world.

Writing to his sister in 1942 to discourage her from 'any voyages to England to marry any Englishman', he declared that 'it has come time to write the obituary of the British Empire. When it reaches the point where it is willing to sacrifice part of the status quo to keep the rest it's gone beyond being old, it's dying — and that is the state of mind England reached some time ago.'[24]

As a teenager he seemed surprisingly unpolitical. There is little evidence that any of the stirring events of the Depression and the New Deal found a response in him. Mass unemployment and bitter industrial disputes passed him by. All had been pre-ordained by Father — Young Joe would be the family politician. That left Jack to be the family playboy and dilettante, writer and academic. During World War II his mother told her family that Jack 'thinks it would be good for Joe's political career if he died for the grand old flag, although I don't believe he feels that is absolutely necessary'. What did grip his imagination was the crisis in Europe in the late 1930s.[25]

In contrast to his older brother, Jack was not a hearty, aggressive type. At least publicly, in the early days, he was reserved, almost shy. His first biographer, James MacGregor Burns, later wondered if this was a reaction to his grandfather, 'that he grew up very sensitive to the impression' that Honey Fitz had created. According to Burns, John F. Fitzgerald was the picture of the 'clowning-type, sentimental-type, blarney-type Irishman'. In fact, Kennedy had a deep love and regard for his grandfather. Nevertheless, when he was in the midst of his political career, he privately declared that the day of the old-time politician was long past. The fact that he did not appear to be a professional politician turned out to be a great asset.

After spending some time with his father in London and travelling in Europe, Jack returned to the US in

September 1939. This trip marked his first time in Ireland: he was to return for five additional visits. On this occasion he flew a Pan American Clippership from Foynes in County Limerick (since replaced by Shannon airport), probably having travelled there on a connecting flight from London. He resumed his studies at Harvard and wrote his senior thesis on the reasons why Britain failed to re-arm in face of the growing threat from Germany. After a complete professional re-write, it was published as *Why England Slept*, and was a best-seller in 1940 (Daddy buying a few thousand copies certainly helped; he was to do the same thing with Jack's next book).[26]

After graduating from Harvard in June 1940, Jack attended Stanford Graduate Business School in California in the Autumn semester as a casual student. One young man to whom Kennedy became attached recalled that Jack liked him because he assumed that this student was part of the established social set in New York which Kennedy 'didn't know and couldn't get to know, because he was an Irish guy from Boston — he was a "mick".' He believed that the apparently casual Jack felt this social disability and reacted to it with political ambition — he'll show them. Another student remembered the professor in the single course that Kennedy audited who was strongly opposed to stock market buccaneers like Joe Kennedy and often commented: 'The Irish potato famine of the 1840s was the greatest disaster that ever struck the US.' Apparently this comment was not made while Kennedy was in attendance, but he probably heard about it.[27]

At the beginning of 1941 he wrote his first newspaper article, which dealt with the controversy between Britain and Ireland concerning the British demand for Irish naval and air facilities. Kennedy provided an informed, thoughtful and balanced treatment of the subject, which was more than fair to the Irish side. The article was written for the International News Service, part of the Hearst newspaper empire, and appeared in the *New York Journal American*, the Boston *Sunday Advertiser* and other Hearst papers in February 1941 (*Document 1*). The introduction to the article claimed that Jack had been in Ireland in the period 1939-40, this referring to his otherwise unnoted flight out of Foynes.[28]

As is well known, Kennedy served as a PT boat commander in the South Pacific during World War II. According to one of his fellow officers, Kennedy, although a graduate of an Ivy League college, was not accepted socially by other Ivy League officers, who saw him as an 'upstart Irishman'. A fellow officer told him that he had heard his father speak on the radio and 'was surprised that he didn't speak like the rest of the Irish trash from Boston'. This remark made Kennedy furious and he later told a friend that he wanted to punch the officer in the nose. Was his anger caused by the appearance of a slight to his father, a reflection of his grandfathers or on Irish-Americans in general? Another officer, Johnny Ives, recalled that Kennedy told him of the difficulties that the Irish encountered in Boston.

When his boat was sunk by a Japanese destroyer, he became a war hero. A reporter on hand filed a story which began: 'The luck of the Irish and some first class skill brought lanky Lt. J.G. John F. Kennedy, son of former Ambassador Joseph Kennedy, and ten of his torpedo boat mates back from a brush with the Japanese and death today.' Back in the US on leave, he wrote a friend, 'Tell Moriarity [a member of his crew] I talked with his folks and they sounded fine. Spent the weekend in Boston where I gave an exhibition of talking where I should have been listening.' In writing to another friend, Paul 'Red' Fay, Kennedy referred to himself as an Irishman:

> I'm sorry I haven't come through with a report on how the Irishman is doing. Frankly, Red, it's a bit slow. Either they haven't read the August issue of the *Readers Digest* [describing his exploits] or something, for every time I introduce Kula Gulf into the circle (in itself no mean feat) the conversation just seems to pick itself up and walk into a corner and die.[29]

As a result of injuries suffered during the war, Kennedy was discharged from the US Navy early in 1945 and for a short period was a journalist for the Hearst newspaper chain. He travelled to Britain to report on the general election of June 1945. While there he made his second of six visits to Ireland. His father was most interested in Jack going there. Having talked to a State Department official who strongly approved and who informed Eamon de Valera about this, Joe cabled his son: 'Think it most important as do important people here that you go and cover the situation minutely. All papers and magazines will be vitally interested I know.' Jack travelled to Dublin in July where he stayed at the US legation and interviewed Eamon de Valera, Richard Mulcahy, Frank Gallagher and, apparently, James Dillon. After attending a session of Dáil Éireann, he wrote a balanced and fair-minded article about the partition of Ireland and the constitutional status of the state. The article had little sense of Kennedy being on Irish soil and could have as easily been written from newspaper accounts in London. It appeared in the Hearst newspapers later that month and did not get the attention anticipated by his father (*Document 2*). Kennedy probably would have stayed longer in Dublin but his father had also arranged for him to travel to the Potsdam conference in Berlin at this time.[30]

Following the death of his brother, Jack Kennedy began a political career, with a mighty push from his father. He probably wanted to do this in any case, but Joe Jr. always came first in the eyes of Joe Sr. Had young Joe pursued a full-fledged political career, with the US presidency as the objective, his younger brother surely would have been involved in the process, just as Bobby was with Jack. As early as 1942 Jack was thinking about shooting for the top himself. Writing to him in February 1942 his very good friend Inga Arvad referred to his secret desire to 'be a White-House Man'. She thought he could make it because he was, among other things, 'brainy and Irish-shrewd'. Moreover, 'You have more than even your ancestors and yet you haven't lost the tough hide of the Irish potatoes.'[31]

Even before the death of young Joe, however, the father had Jack sized up by his politically experienced cousin. Joe Kane reported that Jack 'has poise, a fine Celtic map, a most engaging smile'; moreover, 'There is something original about your young daredevil.' He later told Joe: 'Your Jack is worth a king's ransom.' Young Kennedy could be presented as the prototype of the new breed of politician for the ethnic (read Irish) voters. 'Brother,' commented Kane, 'would they puff and go for that line.'

In preparing the way for his boy, Joe Kennedy left nothing to chance. According to Kane, he was a major contributor to Congressman James M. Curley's successful campaign for mayor of Boston in 1945, thus creating a House vacancy the next year. It was more than a coincidence that Kennedy's intimate friend, Joe Timulty was campaign manager and that John F. Fitzgerald endorsed his old rival in that race.

Young Jack set out to establish himself in Boston; at that time about the only people he knew there were his grandparents In his first public address, 'England, Ireland and Germany: Victor Neutral, Vanquished', which he first delivered in November 1945, he described at great length his experiences in Dublin earlier that year (*Document 3*).

When he ran for Congress in 1946 he entered the arena in one of the most heavily Irish districts in the country. In that first campaign all of his family joined in — save Kathleen, Marchioness of Hartington, who kept out of sight. He had an Irish name and a strong Boston family background, plus good looks, intelligence and lots of campaign money and, as James Michael Curley predicted, he won in a walk. One of the features of the Kennedy campaign was house-parties (fully paid for with Kennedy money) at which Joseph F. Leahy sang Irish songs. Leahy recalled how much Kennedy enjoyed the songs: 'There was one song that he loved in particular; it was *Danny Boy.* . . . Oh, he used to love *Macushla* and *When Irish Eyes Are Smiling* and *Killarney* and songs like that.' Leahy later provided an impromptu, curb-side performance of *Danny Boy* for Jackie on the night of the Inauguration in 1961.

Dave Powers, his long-time political aide, commented about this election: Kennedy had

> a pride in his bearing that appealed to every Irishman who was beginning to feel a little embarrassed about the sentimental, corny style of the typical Irish politician. As the Irish themselves were becoming more middle-class, they wanted a leader to reflect their upward mobility.

He also said that in this first campaign Kennedy spoke every word at public meetings as though he was having a tooth pulled out! The historian William G. Carleton, who met all the Kennedys in 1941, believed that Joe Jr. was clearly the 'political type', whereas Jack possessed greater ultimate political appeal. He observed: 'John's mind was more penetrating and dispassionate, and he did not fit the stereotype of the politician, particularly the Irish politician.'[32]

To be surrounded by and embedded in a mass of ordinary Irish and Italian-American people must have had some impact on his thinking about his ethnic relationship. In any case, during his first trip to Europe after his election — in 1947 — he visited Ireland for the third time.

On 1 August Kennedy announced that he would travel to Ireland in September to make a personal study of food and fuel shortages: 'Reports from Eire indicate that conditions, although improved, are still critical.' With the US sending large quantities of food to various countries, 'it may be that we should give the Irish considerable assistance.' He said he planned to meet with Prime Minister de Valera and other government officials to discuss the situation. At the time he was making this statement, Clement A. Norton, one of his Boston political cronies, was reporting from Dublin that there seemed to be plenty of food available. But there were serious problems, caused by crop failures due to torrential rains and a severe winter and by restricted coal exports from England.

Kennedy had another reason for going to Ireland: 'I'm going to travel around the country and talk to the people. And I'm going to find out where the Kennedys and the Fitzgeralds came from.' He said that his grandfather Honey Fitz had told him that side of the family came from Tipperary!

He arrived at Shannon on 1 September and spent most of his three weeks in Ireland with his sister Kathleen at Lismore Castle in County Waterford, which belonged to the Devonshires, the parents of her late husband. Kit apparently had become completely anglicised, something that was incomprehensible to her father. Her purpose in Ireland was not to trace the family tree. For this occasion, she had invited a very grand group of English person-alities. He spent much time talking with her about her plans to marry another rich Anglo-Irish nobleman, this one being already married. Kennedy went to Dublin on 10 September and spent an hour discussing economic and financial problems with de Valera. Apparently that was the extent of his investigation into economic con-ditions in the 'Oul Sod'.

He also made another trip — to the Kennedys of Dunganstown, County Wexford. Before he left America he had solicited a letter from his aunt and godmother Loretta Kennedy Connelly about its location. One day he decided to drive to it. He surely mentioned this intention to his sister and invited her to join him. In any event, his travelling companion was Pamela Digby Churchill, ex-wife of Randolph Churchill, who noted that Kennedy was excited about the visit, but he asked her 'not to make a big thing of it' to his sister.[33]

Driving in Kathleen's new American station wagon, Jack and Pamela arrived in Dunganstown after several hours of travel. He visited the homes of two relatives. He was directed first to the home of James Kennedy, where he met Jim, his wife and four children. Although he had a brother and a sister living in Long Island, Jim Kennedy was not aware of anyone emigrating to America earlier. Then he recalled a Patrick Kennedy from Boston who visited around 1912. 'That was my grandfather', replied

Jack Kennedy. He stayed about an hour, had tea, took photos of the family and asked about the family history. The Kennedys of Dunganstown remember him as 'a frail, thin young man of most unassuming disposition'.

He was then directed down the road to May Ryan, Jim's sister, who lived in the original Kennedy cottage. According to Pamela Churchill, when they showed up in front of the Kennedy thatched cottage, the people there could not figure out who he was or, more importantly, what he wanted. Mary Ryan was the granddaughter of Patrick Kennedy's brother James and she had married her second cousin, James Ryan, a grandson of another brother, John. They offered him the luxury of fresh butter and eggs, scarce commodities in post-war Europe. Kennedy appeared to be in need of nourishment: Mrs. Ryan recalled that 'he didn't look well at all'. According to Pamela Churchill, 'Jack kept pressing on about his ancestors going to America and so on, trying to make the link. They said, well, they had an uncle who went to America — Long Island — in 1920 and made good. He had a roadhouse! Jack said he didn't think that was the one. He could never make the link, but he seemed to be satisfied that they were some relation.' Kennedy said that Jim Ryan remembered a visit of Patrick Kennedy before the Great War.

Mary Ryan later recalled that Patrick, 'the Senator', had written letters and sent a photograph to the family. During his one hour visit Kennedy noted amidst the chickens, ducks and pigs a group of beautiful pale blond tow-headed children. He gave them a ride around the village in the new American station wagon he was driving. He took photographs, which he later sent to them, of his new-found 'third cousins'. Then as he drove away, 'in a flow of nostalgia and sentiment', his travelling companion, declared, 'Just like Tobacco Road'. He said later that 'she had not understood at all the magic of the afternoon' and later still, 'I felt like kicking her out of the car.' Jack returned to Lismore anxious to tell Kathleen what he had discovered, but he arrived late for dinner at the castle and Kathleen, obviously irritated, simply inquired, 'Did they have a bathroom?' At dinner, he looked around the room and 'thought about the cottage where my cousins lived, and I said to myself, "What a contrast."' Rose Kennedy and her daughter Patricia arrived in Ireland on 23 September and spent their time with Kathleen in Lismore; Dunganstown was not added to their itinerary.

Neither he nor any member of his family had any further contact with the Kennedys of Dunganstown for many years (not even a Christmas card or the like). This was not a port of call for the globe-trotting clan. According to the *New Ross Standard* (11 November 1960), 'The Kennedys and the Ryans heard no more of their visitor and had almost forgotten the incident until Kennedy became a candidate for President.' In the late 1950s, to assist his first biographer, Kennedy again turned to his aunt Loretta for help: could she recall what he had told her of this fleeting visit — 'the names of some of the relatives . . . what the countryside looked like, and how I would have gotten there.' She remembered very little, so he must have got the information from other relatives. But he had not forgotten Pamela Churchill's remark about Tobacco Road. His immediate family retained only a scant memory of this visit. Rose Kennedy wrote in her diary about children walking by the castle grounds 'in their bare legs and shabby shoes and torn coats but shining rosy faces'. Aunt Loretta reminded Jack that he told another relative about the 'tow-headed children' in Dunganstown (*Document 4*).[34]

Almost all of the Kennedy siblings apparently visited Dublin in the Summer of 1949. Frank More O'Ferrell, a London friend from the late 1930s, rented a house in Dublin for the week of the Dublin Horse Show. According to O'Ferrell, a bunch of the Kennedy children, including Jack and Bobby, stayed with him. They were not there principally for the show-jumping: 'They wanted to come to Ireland and to see what it was like again after all that time,' observed O'Ferrell, 'and have a general get together. . . . We had a really hilarious week.'[35]

As a new congressman, Kennedy's interests were eclectic. He gave considerable attention to labour and housing matters and foreign affairs. At one time he conducted a one-man, self-appointed survey of US military facilities — while the House was in session. He had one of the worst — if not the worst — attendance records of any congressman in the six years he served there. Nevertheless, he managed to defeat Henry Cabot Lodge for a senate seat in 1952. Running against the Eisenhower tide, with Ike coming to Boston on the eve of the election to help Lodge, Kennedy won by 70,000 votes. In accounts of this election, Kennedy's victory has been treated as exceptional. In fact, three other state-wide Democratic candidates (for state treasurer, auditor and secretary of state) achieved a similar result. Kennedy secured the base Democratic vote in that election, no mean feat in itself.

It was also a family grudge match: in 1916 Lodge's grandfather had narrowly defeated Honey Fitz for the same seat. The Lodges were of the Boston Brahmins, the kind of people who refused social acceptance to the rising Irish Catholics, like the Kennedys. Rose Kennedy declared, 'At last the Kennedys have evened the score!' Fitzgerald, who had died just two years earlier, would have loved to have been present on this occasion. To pay for an election bet, Kennedy at a victory party sang, in bad voice, all of the stanzas *Sweet Adeline*, Fitzgerald's signature song. Indeed, the Kennedys were to defeat the Lodges in two subsequent elections — in 1960 and 1962. Kennedy's running mate in 1952, Governor Paul A. Dever, declared that Jack 'is the first Irish Brahmin' and the abrasive Robert Kennedy 'is the last Irish Puritan'.[36]

His interest in Ireland at this time would appear to be limited. When Eamon de Valera came to Boston in 1948 as part of a world tour for Irish unification, young Congressman Kennedy was at the airport at midnight to give him an enthusiastic welcome. He supported a resolution put forward by Rep. John E. Fogarty of Rhode Island which supported a united Ireland. In September 1950 he made brief statement to the House Foreign Affairs Committee:

> In view of our American tradition of liberty and democratic processes and in view of the glorious pages which men and women of Irish descent have written in our Nation's history, I believe that justice will be served in great measure if all of the people of Ireland are given the opportunity to choose their own form of government. The free plebiscite, as suggested in the resolution under consideration, will give the Irish people that opportunity.

His statement to the full House was short, almost curt, compared to the orations of other proponents (*Documents 5, 6*).

When he ran for the Senate in 1952 he made use of this position in literature directed at Irish organisations. As a member of the Senate, Kennedy was the co-sponsor (with Jacob Javitts of New York and Everett Dirksen of Illinois) of a similar resolution. This proposed a vote of all the people of Ireland, supervised by the United Nations, on the question of unification.

In seeking the support of other senators, Kennedy declared: 'We have traditionally tried to help peoples who were seeking unification or seeking a legitimate expression of their desire for self-determination as they see it.' The resolution received only a small amount of support in the Senate and Kennedy did not carry the matter to the public platform or write articles about it. To Thomas J. Kiernan, later Irish Ambassador to the US, Kennedy's support of the resolution was simply political opportunism. Thus, there is no evidence that he was deeply committed to this position or was prepared to do anything about it. It occurs to me, however, that Kennedy was completely committed to the pursuit of the presidency and he realised it would be harmful to be seen as being a strong supporter of Irish causes. Moreover, I would suspect that word of this strategy was sent out in Irish-American political circles, which Joe Kennedy, for one, knew intimately: if you want one of our own to make it to the top, don't expect him to be yammering about Irish unification, etc. After all, the Kennedys left nothing to chance in that carefully plotted campaign, and it worked.[37]

As a young, articulate politician of Irish extraction, Kennedy was invited to address Irish organisations around St. Patrick's Day in the 1950s. He did this in several cities around the country, which was helpful in meeting people in various places. His addresses were very well constructed — witty, sensitive, literate, including measured praise for the Irish combined with a wider theme — usually freedom as the objective of all peoples. Bishop John Wright of Worcester, Massachusetts provided him with one of the speeches. Ted Sorenson recalled that his first speech-writing assignment for Kennedy was to write a St. Patrick's Day address, 'a phenomenon unknown to my background'.

All of them had the same format. He would begin by asking his audience to 'remember' the three requests granted St. Patrick by the Angel of the Lord:

> That the weather should always be fair on his special day to allow the faithful to attend the services [not Mass!] of the Church; secondly that every Thursday and every Saturday twelve souls of Irish people should be freed from the pains of Hell; and third, that no outlander should ever rule over Ireland.

He would continue:

> I have not heard a weather report from the Emerald Isle tonight, but I am certain that no rain fell — officially. I have no doubt that twelve Irishmen have been freed from the nether regions this very [night]. In fact, your [president, toastmaster] tells me he thinks he saw several of them here tonight.

Then came the business of foreigners ruling in Ireland. On one occasion he acknowledged the reality that Northern Ireland was part of the United Kingdom: 'An outlander still rules, in part. But nevertheless, at least the country of Eire is free and independent.' He usually avoided this matter by simply saying 'no outlander rules over Eire; and the Irish people are celebrating this day in peace and in liberty.'

He would then proceed to extol the virtues of various Irish patriots — from Arthur O'Connor to Roger Casement. A bit of his favourite poetry paid tribute to Irish exiles: 'War-battered dogs are we, gnawing a naked bone; fighters in every land and clime — (for) every cause but our own.'

Then very Kennedyish oratory:

> I do not maintain that the Irish were the only race
> to display extraordinary devotion to liberty, or the
> only people to struggle unceasingly for their national
> independence. History proves otherwise. But the
> special contribution of the Irish, I believe — the
> emerald thread that runs throughout the tapestry of
> their past — has been the constancy, the endurance,
> the faith that they displayed through endless cen-
> turies of foreign oppression — centuries in which
> even the most rudimentary religious and civil rights
> were denied to them.

He drew a parallel between the long and ultimately
successful Irish struggle for independence and the
contemporary revolt of Asian and Arab countries against
European imperialism. Was this all blather and blarney,
to be put aside once it was said? Kennedy was not the
kind of person who was given to hyperbole and empty
rhetoric (*Document 8*).

Aside from the St. Patrick's Day occasions, Kennedy
almost never made any public allusions to Ireland; he
did not draw any parallels between that country's long
struggle for self-government and what was happening elsewhere. Not that he didn't know about it! When in a 1957
Senate debate another member drew a parallel between
Poland and Ireland, Kennedy was quick to respond:

> In the first place, the Irish revolt lasted 700 years,
> and the Easter rebellion was one of a long series of
> disasters which befell the Irish people before they
> became independent. I do not wish to have the
> Poles undergo the same experience, especially
> under conditions of modern totalitarianism . . .[38]

At the age of 36, Kennedy finally got married, to Jacqueline Lee Bouvier, a 24-year-old socialite. She was the daughter of 'Black Jack' Bouvier, a New York stockbroker who lost his fortune in the Crash of 1929, but was supposedly of distinguished French lineage. To the Kennedys and to most others, therefore, Jackie was 'French', with a knowledge of the language and culture of France that passed muster with the likes of Charles de Gaulle. For many Irish people French culture, religion and government were attractive alternatives to dreaded Anglophilism.

In fact, Jackie was more Irish than French. Her mother, Janet Norton Lee, gave the impression that she was one of the Lees of Maryland, but her grandparents were famine Irish immigrants who settled in New York city, specifically in the Irish slum of the Lower East Side. Her father, James T. Lee, made a fortune in real estate and decided to move up socially. When there was company in their mansion, his mother-in-law, with her brogue, was relegated to sitting at the top of the stairs to hear what was going on. Her cousin, John H. Davis, says that Jackie 'did everything possible to hide her Irish background' from Jack and 'studiously kept her mother's relatives from meeting him'. This included crusty, politically-reactionary Grandfather Lee, who lived to the 1970s. Truman Capote later said that a bit of Irish grit was what the Bouviers needed. (Jack also thought she had money, which she did not.) Two years earlier she had visited Ireland, which she found most romantic. When she asked Jack how someone as Irish as himself could be so interested in English history, he just smiled and said, 'But that's the way it is.'[39]

By this time, her mother was long married to Hugh D. Auchincloss, a rich stockbroker with a mansion in

Newport, Rhode Island. The wedding was a high society affair, but Jack was not overly concerned. The day before the wedding he brought two of his friends, Paul 'Red' Fay and John Galvin, the latter if not the former, 'looking more Irish than Paddy's pig', to play at a near-by exclusive golf course. Mrs. Achincloss was furious: non-members could only play there accompanied by a member! Referring to Newport's upper crust, Jack told his pals, 'I'm afraid that they feel that their worst fears are being realised. The invasion by the Irish Catholic hordes into one of the last strongholds of America's socially elite is being led by two chunky red-haired friends of the groom.' Jackie told a friend that she was terrified about marrying into 'that Irish stronghold of Kennedys'. A few months after their marriage Jackie wrote a poem about her husband. Not destined to find its way into anthologies, it nevertheless met with an enthusiastic response from the clan. After celebrating Jack's Massachusetts heritage, it continued:

> He would call New England his place and his creed
> But part he was of an alien breed
> Of a breed that had laughed on Irish hills
> And heard the voices of Irish rills.
>
> The lilt of that green land danced in his blood
> Tara, Killarney, a magical flood
> That surged in the depth of his too proud heart
> And spiked the punch of New England so tart. . .[40]

In 1955 Kennedy made his fourth visit to Ireland. Jackie made the arrangements. While in Dublin in 1951 she had met Father Joseph Leonard, a Vincentian priest at All Hallowes College, who was both a Francophile and a person of deep literary knowledge. As a result, they became close friends and corresponded until Father Leonard's death in the late 1960s. Jackie wanted Jack to meet Father Leonard; Jack said he would come to Dublin if a speaking engagement could be arranged. Thus the Kennedys arrived for a three-day visit on 30 September 1955. His first appointment was lunch with Liam Cosgrave, Minister for External Affairs. Cosgrave observed that Kennedy had a keen interest in Irish history and politics, including the matter of partition. Then there was the lecture, arranged at All Hallowes, with students for the neighbouring seminary of St. Patrick's being added to the audience. Kennedy spoke about the conditions in Poland, where he had just been. He was also anxious for questions about Ireland and Catholicism, as though he wanted to test his knowledge and ideas of these matters before an Irish audience.

Jackie and himself also spent an evening or two with journalists in Dublin pubs. For a short period after the war Kennedy had been a journalist and he enjoyed the company of newspapermen. Jackie telephoned to invite them to meet the Senator. Very few declined, although one who did lived to regret it. The newspapermen noted that he was an avid student of Joyce, O'Casey and Shaw. Only one newspaper noted the visit, and this briefly (Document 7). This was to be his last visit to Ireland for eight years. His campaign for the presidency was about to commence, and in that quest Detroit was more important than Dunganstown.[41]

Chapter Two

THE PRESIDENCY

The presidency of the United States of America is the greatest electoral prize in the world. The Kennedys and Fitzgeralds had made politics their profession for over three quarters of a century when their family representative sought and won this office. As a congressman, John F. Fitzgerald had been in the world of Washington, DC. In the last years of his life at a family gathering Honey Fitz proposed a toast, with young Jack sitting across from him: 'To a future President of the United States, my grandson, John Fitzgerald Kennedy.' Joseph Kennedy had been deeply involved in the presidency of Franklin Roosevelt in the 1930s. To him, the White House was the family goal. Young Joe was referred to as the family standard-bearer. When he died in the war, Jack assumed his place. In 1946 a delegation of politicians urged Joe to withdraw his young, inexperienced son from the race for Congress; Kennedy told them that Jack would be elected president 14 years later. He was.

Kennedy made his first sortie into national politics when he sought the vice-presidential nomination in 1956. As part of this quest, he strongly supported the presidential nomination of Adlai Stevenson. To bolster his claim for the second spot, Kennedy's staff prepared an analysis which showed that a northern, urban Catholic vice-presidential candidate could attract traditional ethnic

Democratic support, which had been drifting from its historic base.

When Kennedy narrowly failed to get the nomination he began spreading the story that this was a blessing in disguise because if he had been on the ticket that went down to defeat, his career would have been effectively hobbled. In seeking the vice-presidential slot, however, Kennedy knew full well that Stevenson's chances of defeating Dwight D. Eisenhower were extremely remote, so Kennedy wanted the position for self-promotion. If Kennedy was on the ticket no one would have blamed a big-city Democratic like himself for causing the defeat. But the Kennedys were fond of funny, self-serving stories, and this was one of them.[1]

To bolster his claim to be a serious candidate for the presidency, Kennedy needed to be re-elected to the Senate in 1958 with an impressive majority. His father, who prided himself on his knowledge of grass-roots ethnic relations, violently objected to the principal campaign slogan that was planned for this campaign: 'Make Your Vote Count'. Old Joe believed this would offend Italian-Americans, a vital constituency, who would view it as Irish triumphalism. Kennedy was running on a slate that included Governor Foster Furcolo, the first Italian-American to reach the top level in state politics. The slogan was seen by Kennedy Senior as implying that a vote for Jack would be more valuable than one for Furcolo. The slogan was dropped and Kennedy won re-election by a record margin.

It may seem surprising that someone with Kennedy's ethnic awareness should show apparent insensitivity to the huge Italian community in Massachusetts. Kennedy was dutiful in backing aid to Italy, etc., but there was not a single Italian-American who was a prominent member of his staff either when he was a congressman or senator. Almost every one of them (with the exception of Ted Sorensen) was Irish. Kennedy had a difficult, abrasive relationship with Furcolo (who attended Yale under the name Furcolow). The problem really was not ethnic rivalry, but many people saw some of that in it. Rather, it was a case of two ambitious young men who got in each other's way. For public consumption, the two patched up their differences for the 1956 and 1958 elections.

Kennedy also took a casual attitude towards residence. Elected congressman in 1946 from a hotel room; he then rented a two-bedroomed apartment in a respectable but otherwise non-descript block of flats. All of his siblings were registered to vote from the place, described as having the shabby furniture of a bus terminal waiting-room. Upon his election as senator, then after he was married and finally when he ran for president, Kennedy, a millionaire, was urged to acquire a more appropriate residence. But he saw no need for it, as he stayed there infrequently. There was another consideration in his mind: 'What about Mr. Murphy?' Janitor Joe Murphy and his wife from their basement apartment prepared the occasional breakfast for Jack just the way he liked it — orange juice in a certain size glass, eggs just right. Clem Norton, for one, could not figure it out.

The most notable aspect of John F. Kennedy as a candidate was the fact that he was a Catholic, the first Catholic to be a real presidential possibility since Governor Al Smith in 1928. He was also seen as young, handsome, articulate and Irish in origin. In his quest for the presidency, he assembled an inner group of advisors and operatives who, almost to a man, were of the same background as himself. O'Donnell, Maguire, Hartigan, Sullivan, O'Hara and O'Gorman: One of them ruefully shook his head and muttered, 'Wait till they read our names — "Hibernian Hall all over again".' After his election this group was labelled the 'Irish Mafia', a term Kennedy disliked.[2]

Kennedy set out to widen his political base well beyond what it had been as a congressman and senator. To demonstrate his broadminded views, in a book review he had some appreciative words for progressive Republicans in Massachusetts. In a booklet published in 1958, *A Nation of Immigrants*, he had something good to say about every ethnic group. The Irish? These he treated with humour, but also with insight. The 'bold, imaginative' Irish, he declared, had the distinction of being the only group to have a political party organised against them — the American Party, or no-nothing movement, of the early 1850s. He noted the great Irish contribution in building the transportation network, including the Erie canal (which easily could have been called the Eire canal). In support of a broadly-based immigration policy, he quoted the ironic words of Peter Finlay Dunne's Mr. Dooley who declared: 'because I'm here first, [it was time] we put our back again' th' open dure an' keep out th' savage horde.' He also included some words of the Irish-born poet John Boyle O'Reilly who had deplored 'organised charity, scrimped and iced, in the name of a cautious, statistical Christ'. Curiously, he did not mention Irish involvement in two of their most prominent fields — politics and government.[3]

Quoting O'Reilly brings to mind James M. Curley, the old nemesis of the Fitzgerald-Kennedys, who always included a bit of O'Reilly poetry in his speeches. While Kennedy was proclaiming new days and new challenges in his pursuit of the presidency in the late 1950s, Curley made a remarkable if non-political comeback in public esteem. In 1956, Edwin O'Connor published his novel *The Last Hurrah* which painted a sympathetic picture of an aged Irish city boss, the great James Michael, thinly-disguised. The book was made into an excellent film, starring Spenser Tracy as Frank Skeffington. Curley followed this up with his autobiography, *I'd Do It Again!* Undoubtedly the Kennedys were not amused. Curley and Jack Kennedy had just been on opposite sides in a battle for the control of the state party, which Kennedy, of course, won.[4]

To convince the party professionals, particularly the rump of the big city Irish Catholic bosses, that he could win, Kennedy entered almost every presidential primary. Campaigning in Wisconsin — a crucial state — on 17 March 1960 he toured a strongly Lutheran, rural area. Driving along with the press following he was confronted by a group of nuns along the road. Would he stop to acknowledge their greeting or ignore this potentially harmful photo opportunity? He stopped. Teddy White, one of the travelling journalists, thought to himself, now that is gamesmanship! They proudly pinned a large green corsage on him, which he shortly reduced to a mere shred, but that remained. When a rally at the next town proved abortive, he stepped into a bar with his sole local supporter and had a shot of Irish whiskey. He commented to Dave Powers: 'What a hell of a way to spend St. Patrick's Day!'[5]

Kennedy once wondered why Adlai Stevenson, the 1952 and 1956 party nominee, could not get the votes of 'the little old Irish ladies'. For his part, Stevenson, in assessing Kennedy's capacities, commented: 'He has this instinctive feel for politics that these Irish pols have, the Honey Fitzgerald instinct, and it's there and you should never underrate it.' Kennedy's election to the Harvard Board of Overseers in 1957 was seen by his father as a good omen: 'Now I know his religion won't keep him out of the White House. If an Irish Catholic can get elected as an Overseer at Harvard, he can get elected to anything.'

A string of primary victories convinced the big-city politicos that it would be safe and sane to support one of their own. Joe Kennedy had been working on them, with money and personal contact, for years. Kenneth O'Donnell later said that Jack would have been amazed to know what his father had been telling the modern day versions of Grandpa Kennedy. They delivered. The Kennedy family became a feature story in the press. *Time* magazine (11 July 1960) declared: 'The Kennedy clan is as handsome and spirited as a meadow full of Irish thoroughbreds, as tough as a blackthorn shillelagh, as ruthless as Cuchulain, the mythical hero who cast up the hills of Ireland with his sword.'

At the Democratic convention Bobby Kennedy commented to a gathering of southern delegates: 'My, you've got a lot of cantankerous politicians in the south.' A reply came from the audience: 'What the hell do you think you Boston Irish are?' Eugene McCarthy, who believed *he* was the Irish Catholic liberal and intellectual in the party, gave a rousing nomination speech for Stevenson, although he was principally interested in stopping Kennedy (Gene had hopes for the vice-presidential slot). Robert Kennedy later said: 'McCarthy doesn't respect anyone who can't quote as much Aquinas as he.' The Kennedys knew little enough about the Angelic Doctor but a lot about delegate counts. Despite his reservations, McCarthy vigorously campaigned for the national ticket in 1960. Eight years later he came head to head with Bobby.

A victor on the first ballot, Jack returned to his hotel suite to be greeted by his staff with Evelyn Lincoln at the piano playing *When Irish Eyes Are Smiling*.[6]

Richard Nixon later declared in the 1960 election that there was not one Irish candidate but two. Nixon was very proud of his Irish connection through his Milhous background, Germans from the Palatine who migrated to Ireland. He also liked to talk about the Irish ancestry of his wife, the former Thelma Patricia Ryan. When he eventually became President, he visited Ireland, although he did not test his fortunes with public appearances. Nor did he mention this occasion in his memoirs.

According to Mark Levy and Michael Kramer, among others, Kennedy was elected largely due to his ability to pull back urban, ethnic, northern Democratic voters who had voted for Eisenhower. According to their figures, he got 75 per cent of voters of Irish identity. He did as well among Italians and best with those of Slavic background. They believe that Kennedy appealed to Irish voters for two different reasons. Skilled workers were drawn by his pro-labour voting record and their common religion. At least some middle class Irish voted for him 'because he was a symbol of Catholic [and Irish?] success in a WASP world'. The Kennedys have been able to sustain this substantial base among Irish Catholic voters, to a much greater degree than other candidates. Why? 'The Kennedys are more than "one of their own"; they are *the* Irish Catholic family in America; they give glamour and social prominence to an ethnic group which has until very recently been denied acceptance in American society.'[7]

As is well known, religion played a role in the election. Many Catholics voted for Kennedy because not only were the great majority of them Democrats, but — for once — they wanted to see someone of their own religious identity as president. Some Protestants opposed Kennedy for fear of papal domination of American government, and worse. There were a few people who voiced high-minded concerns about the matter of Catholicism and American politics. One of these was Archibold MacLeish, New England Yankee, poet and literary critic, who wrote in *Life* magazine: 'The Irish Catholics, who are among the most persistent and politically powerful advocates of increasing censorship in the US and who are brought up to submit to clerical authority in matters which the American tradition reserves to the individual conscience, are nevertheless among the most fervent of patriots.' Having identified the problem, he continued: 'Only if a separate system of education should be used to perpetuate the historical ignorance and moral obtuseness on which fear of freedom of the mind is based would the danger of the rejection of the American dream from this quarter become serious.' MacLeish obviously did not like the Kennedys, opposing Jack in 1960, Teddy in 1962 and Bobby in 1964, backing losers all along the line. John Kennedy, of course, was not the product of a Catholic education and he effectively addressed Protestant concerns during the campaign.

The narrow victory of John F. Kennedy was widely viewed as a turning point in American history. For many, he was seen as the person to open the doors of political, and, for that matter, social opportunity for the newer people. In Ireland his election was hailed as a triumph of one of the children of the diaspora.[8]

At New Ross in Wexford a bonfire victory celebration was planned for the night of the election, but this was postponed due to the deaths of 26 Irish Army troops serving in a United Nations peace-keeping force in the Congo. The celebration took place on 20 January, inauguration day. Kennedy sent a tape recorded message, in which he told the gathering he would be with them 'in a

matter of weeks or months'. A Kennedy presidential visit
was on the books.

New Ross went all out for the occasion. The local
newspaper declared: 'Scenes of enthusiasm which have
not been surpassed even by the triumphant marchers of
the victorious All Ireland hurling teams in the town were
witnessed by New Ross on Friday night.' First there was
a parade, which included a large banner which declared,
'To JFK, Sláinte 'gus Saol'. Then there were speeches,
which included orations by Col. F. O'Brien, the US
military attaché, who lauded the Irish people for their
courage and determination, and by Brendan Behan, 'the
well-known playwright', who spoke in Irish and English.
In the midst of the speeches Kenndy's taped message
arrived. Finally Monsignor Browne lit a huge bonfire.[9]

Kennedy invited the New England poet Robert Frost
to participate in the inauguration (surely an Irish touch!).
Frost had sent him a congratulatory telegram: 'Great day
for Boston, Democracy, the Puritans and the Irish.' When
asked why he supported Kennedy, Frost, of conservative
bent, declared that 'liberals were people who would not
take their own side in an argument, and they were
agnostics. Since Catholics could not be agnostics, then
they were not liberals.' Furthermore, he liked decisive
people, so he backed Jack. According to Nancy Dickerson,
Frost said Kennedy's inaugural address was Irish because
it sang and had a lilt.

Shortly after the event, Frost said to him: 'You're something of Irish and something of Harvard. Let me advise
you, be more Irish than Harvard. Poetry and power is
the formula for another Augustan Age. Don't be afraid of
power.' When I read that statement, I was galvanised:
this was exactly what I wanted and hoped for! Others
reacted differently. William Manchester declared that

Kennedy had such a weak perception of any Irish heritage that he did not know how to respond to Frost's advise. Ralph G. Martin comments:

> Kennedy was only somewhat Harvard and even less Irish. The Irish was there in the wit and the wink and in some of his defiance and pride. The Harvard was there in his respect for brains and knowledge. But basically, in temperament, he was an English Whig.

Kennedy clearly understood what Frost was advising. At the bottom of a note to Frost, he wrote, 'Power All the Way.'

A year later the Jesuit periodical *America* declared that the Irish and Harvard parts of Kennedy were running neck and neck, but added that 'in his deepest marrow' he was 'an Irish-American from Boston.'[10]

During Kennedy's presidency, there was a huge influx of Irish-Americans into the White House and government agencies. The journalist Nancy Dickerson recalls that the Kennedy White House 'was Irish, which made it fun, and blended with the spirit of Harvard and the patina of Jackie's finishing schools, the mixture was intoxicating.'

Reading down the list of oral history interviews in the Kennedy Library shows clearly that a large number of these people were rewarded for helping to make him president. Although he did not like the term Irish Mafia, the executive office was loaded with these people, from chief of staff (Kenny O'Donnell), legislative liaison (Larry O'Brien) and personal aide (Dave Powers) to head of the motor pool (Jack McCabe) to general go-for (Muggsy O'Leary). There was a plane-load of them for his 1963 visit to Ireland. For professional politicians, life at the top was wonderful.

The inner circle of political advisors were all Irish-Americans; on the other hand, his intellectual and policy advisors were not. Kennedy was aware of the need for diversity in his staff. He told Ken O'Donnell:

> If I string along exclusively with Galbraith, and Arthur Schlesinger and Seymour Harris and those other Harvard liberals, they'll fill Washington with wild-eyed ADA people. And if I listen to you and Powers and Bailey and Maguire, we'll have so many Irish Catholics that we'll have to organise a White House Knights of Columbus Council. I can use a few smart Republicans.

In retrospect some Kennedy officials saw the value in balance. Donald Wilson has said: 'God knows, if that administration had been dominated by the Irish Mafia, I think it would have been terrible. On the other hand, I think it would have been ineffective if you were going too much with the professors and the intellectual side.' Adam Yarmolisky had this assessment of the Irish inner-circle:

> The Kenny O'Donnells, Dick Donahue and Larry O'Brien were not policymakers. They solved political problems. They were doers. I don't mean to suggest they were errand runners. They were powerful and effective and very knowledgeable. But they were not policymakers.

Louis Martin, one of Kennedy's black advisors, has said that Kennedy was 'the first really "ethnic" President we've ever had'. Because of his background and experience, Kennedy understood the feelings and needs of the various ethnic groups, although he was slow to grasp the magnitude of the black demand for full civil equality.

Kennedy was now in a position to taunt his friend, journalist Ben Bradlee, about his Boston Yankee background, implying that his kind had rubbed it into the likes of the Kennedys and the Fitzgeralds in past times. Kennedy declared that his family was 100 per cent pure Irish, noting gleefully 'how mongrolized you all are'. When Bradlee told him of his difficulty in getting his daughter into an exclusive dance school, Kennedy roared with laughter — the shoe was now on the other foot! Bradlee commented: 'It's really formidable to see the pleasure the president gets out of this story.' On the other hand, Kennedy told his friend Paul Fay: 'Do you know it is impossible for an Irish Catholic to get into the Somerset Club in Boston? If I moved back to Boston even after being President, it would make no difference.' Fay commented later that Kennedy 'must on brief occasions imagine he saw signs reading: "Help Wanted — Irish Don't Apply".' George Smathers, a Senate friend, observed the same thing. Upon being introduced to Nikita Khrushchev in early 1961, Ken O'Donnell gave the Russian leader no smile but a cold, clear stare, which prompted Kennedy to comment that Khrushchev 'must have thought you were a spy from the IRA'. Kennedy soon saw the utility of this approach: 'Maybe we'd get along better with the Russians if we didn't smile at them so damned much.'[11]

The Irish connection came to the fore in the White House. The Irish Government presented Kennedy with his family coat of arms and pedigree. A group of people in Wexford sent the Kennedys a christening cup to commemorate the birth of their son. Before the White House ceremony at which the Irish Ambassador made the presentation, an assistant press secretary informed all that there should be no mention of the fact that the cup had been transported by Irish International Airlines. No commercials, please. The President obviously did not like to be instructed. At the end of the ceremony

Kennedy returned to the microphone to say: 'By the way, this christening cup was brought courtesy of Irish International Airlines.' He gave the Ambassador a piece of the inaugural podium with inscription for the people of Wexford. Irish political leaders, including Robert Briscoe, Lord Mayor of Dublin, were greeted by the President. St. Patrick's Day was celebrated on a expanded scale. When Jackie Kennedy decided to improve the presidential cuisine (Jack said he preferred fish chowder and chocolate ice cream) by bringing in a French and an Italian chef, there was some public disapproval. Joe Kennedy suggested a response: 'Tell them the President feels that there are so many Irishmen in the White House, the French and Italians ought to be given a chance, too.'[12]

Then there was the matter of the visit to Ireland. This would not be so easy to arrange as Kennedy had envisioned; it would have to be made in conjunction with a serious business trip to Europe. After all, with crises erupting around the world, there was no urgent need for him to go to Ireland. His Ambassador to Ireland, Grant Stockdale, informed the Irish Government in June 1961 that the President's failure to visit the country that year 'did not signify in any way that he was unmindful of the country dear to his heart'. Stockdale told Kennedy about the Ambassador's house in the Phoenix Park: 'Our residence is not simply a residence — it's an institution of grandeur.' Moreover: 'You gave us the jewel of all State Department appointments.' Ambassador Kiernan thought that the selection of Stockdale, a Florida businessman (who was only a short-term appointment) showed Kennedy's 'lack of interest in Ireland certainly at that time'.

At the end of 1961 Kennedy told Stockdale: 'I would like very much to come to Ireland next year, if I can think of a reason which would be sufficiently substantial to warrant a visit.' The Irish Ambassador, Thomas J. Kiernan, a short, peppery older man, told him: 'We're not going to press you to come or to invite you officially, but you're always at home when you come and there won't be any fuss.' Although Kennedy was unable to visit Ireland as soon as he would have liked, he did break up a Congressional logjam concerning the building of a new chancery in Dublin, and Stockdale proposed that Kennedy visit the Irish capital upon its completion in early 1962.[13]

Ireland figured, in a small way, in American foreign policy. Stockdale informed the President in July 1961 of his meetings with Fredrick Boland, Ireland's representative at the United Nations, who as President of the General Assembly had effectively dealt with the disruptions of Nikita Khushchev. 'I must say,' declared Stockdale, 'he certainly is co-operating with you in every manner possible. Of course, I know you realise what I mean without putting it down here.' What was this?

A problem developed in the UN in June 1962 when Ireland joined several other nations in supporting the Indian Government in its approach to the Kashmir question. Kennedy wanted to know why they had abandoned the US position, 'leaving us holding the sack'. Kennedy telephoned Ambassador Kiernan to urge him to get his government to change its position and introduce a US-sponsored resolution in the Security Council, commenting: 'We can't put it forward ourselves without it being knocked and we want Ireland to put it forward. . . . If we can get you to come along, we'll get others . . . .' Kennedy said: 'It's really very important, it's very urgent' and he gave his reasons. According to Kiernan, Kennedy 'in a very clear way . . . summarised the whole eight points again in a sentence each. He has a tremendously vital mind like that — crystal clear.' In New York Boland had already made a commitment to Krisna Menon, the Indian foreign minister, on the matter. He told Kiernan there could be no change in position: 'This is impossible. You can't do this. Krisna Menon spent two hours with me over this business and he'll be wild. And we'll lose... we have a certain friendship with India from the old days, and so on, and we can't do it.' Kiernan telephoned Frank Aiken, the Irish foreign minister. The position was changed — immediately. According to Kiernan, 'When it came direct like that from the President, [Aiken] agreed without demur, no difficulty whatever. We introduced the resolution. It was put through.'

There also was the matter of a sugar quota for Ireland. Kiernan had been trying to get Ireland included in this for the first time. He brought the matter to the attention of Kenneth O'Donnell, who said he'd see what he could do. When Kennedy called with his request, 'quite some time after that', the President said that O'Donnell 'mentioned something to me. I'll look after that'. A new bill suddenly appeared, specifically including Ireland. Kiernan: 'We, for the first time, got in on the sugar market. The *Wall Street Journal* said that it was hard to understand how it happened, but somebody with a large smile in Washington seemed to have been responsible.'[14]

There was also the serious matter of the partition of Ireland and the systematic pattern of discrimination against Irish nationalists in Northern Ireland. As a congressman and senator, Kennedy had given pro-forma support to resolutions in favour of Irish unification, but had never spoken out about the northern situation. As president he heard about it from the Irish Government. Here is Ambassador Kiernan's version about one, obviously early, discussion:

He asked me what could be done. And I said, "Well what do you think is the issue?" And he said, "Well, of course it's an Irish issue." I said, "Well, that is the British line very good. But partition was enforced against the wishes of both parts of Ireland by the British. No country cuts itself in two." And that took him aback. He said, "That's quite true, of course, it is a British issue."

Kiernan declared that it was the British Government that supported and financed the six-county sectarian regime in Northern Ireland. He also told the President that the Irish Government did not expect Kennedy to take a public position on the matter. What it sought was a statement by a British Government spokesman that 'it is not contrary to British interests if Ireland became united'. To Kiernan, that was 'putting it in a very minimum way'. Kennedy responded: 'I can see the British difficulty. It's very hard to say that on account of the past history.' When Kiernan brought up Kennedy's congressional support for the anti-partition resolutions, Kennedy laughed. In Kiernan's view, Kennedy 'was very cold' about the matter and 'was, this is putting it much too extreme but it's no harm to put it like that, apart from his Americanism which was a hundred per cent, was more British than Irish'. Kiernan noted, however, that Kennedy's interest and concern about Ireland grew, particularly as a result of his 1963 visit.[15]

The likelihood of such a policy statement from the British Government at that time was zero. Recently released British cabinet papers show that the British Government completely ignored mounting evidence of political, economic and religious discrimination against the Catholic-nationalist community in Northern Ireland.

It accepted totally the assurances of the unionist administration that these charges were false, exaggerated, outdated or all three.[16]

Frank Aiken also talked with Kennedy about the matter of Northern Ireland. He later commented that he found Kennedy 'had an interest in Ireland and would like to do anything he could for it'. He also said, 'I would like to have seen him be a bit more active in getting a solution for partition. We urged him to do it. He perhaps did it quietly but he didn't disclose that fact.' He concluded with a cautious statement: 'I hope, however, I have no reason to believe that he didn't say something in private to the British that it was time that this anachronism should be cleared up.' When Kennedy was in Ireland, President Eamon de Valera discussed the matter with him. De Valera later told his biographer, T. P. O'Neill, that he hoped Kennedy could do something about the North in his second term. Obviously he had some grounds for believing that Kennedy might move on this matter. There is no evidence that Kennedy raised this matter with Harold Macmillan or any other British official. There is also no evidence of any change in British Government policy concerning Northern Ireland until the eruption of violence in the late 1960s.[17]

In the meantime, the President's youngest brother, Edward, made a visit to Ireland in February 1962. Positioning himself to run for his brother's old senate seat, 'Teddy', a hearty, vigorous type, and something of a surrogate, had a warm and lively reception in Wexford during February. The trip did not meet with the approval of one writer in the *Irish Independent*:

> Why is he coming to Ireland? He's coming because later this year he is due to be involved in a political fight back home in Massachusetts. He is playing the

political game in what has now come to be known
as the Kennedy method. You do not spend your time
in campaigning in your own little patch. . . . You go
out into the world far far afield, hit the headlines,
hit the American voters in the right way.

Kiernan passed on to Dublin what he said was a comment
by an unnamed State Department official:

[Kennedy] pulled out all the stops and one could
almost find the pages in Bob Considine [*It's the Irish!*,
popular celtic lore] from which he took notes. What
a pity somebody did not ask him the pertinent question, "What is President Kennedy doing for Ireland?"

Ask not what. . . . Teddy returned to tell his family of his
warm-hearted reception, and he won the election.[18]

The matter of the presidential visit was raised again
by Matthew McCloskey, the new US Ambassador to
Ireland. Writing to the Secretary of State in January 1963,
he reminded him that 'you would try to arrange a day or
two stop-off in Ireland'. Since Kennedy would be running
for re-election in 1964, the visit would have to come
soon. All along Kennedy had been gently reminded of
his commitment by Dorothy Tubridy, an Irish family
friend then living in Washington, who told him: 'I'll
persecute you' until he went. When he made his plans,
he called her to the White House: 'You are the first
person to know.' The visit would be in conjunction with
a European tour: first to Germany, then Ireland, Britain
(briefly) and Italy. According to Ben Bradlee, Kennedy
was keenly interested in this trip, 'especially his visit to
Ireland. This was the part that he really looks forward
to. The rest of the trip is political. Ireland is pure heart.'

According to his account, Kenneth O'Donnell, the
White House chief of staff, reacted to the news as if it

was a bolt out of the blue. He told Kennedy: 'There's no reason for you to go to Ireland. It would be a waste of time. It wouldn't do you much good politically. You've got all the Irish votes in this country that you'll ever get. If you go to Ireland, people will say that it's just a pleasure trip.' When he persisted in his objections, Kennedy closed the discussion: 'Kenny, let me remind you of something. I am the President of the United States, not you. When I say I want to go to Ireland, it means that I'm going to Ireland. Make the arrangements.'

At first he planned only a short visit, limited to Dublin, but upon the urging of Dorothy Tubridy that 'he should see more of the country and spread himself, so to speak, more so that the people in other parts of the country would be so delighted to have him too', he agreed to an expanded itinerary. When he informed the Irish Ambassador of the proposed visit, Kiernan said any arrangement was agreeable and that he could 'come and have a comfortable rest'. That was not Kennedy's intention:

> I don't want to rest in Ireland. I want to go around and meet people. I want to meet plenty of people. I don't want to stay in Dublin. I don't want too many official receptions. I don't want any of the stuff shirt arrangements, if I can avoid it. Just to meet people. But it certainly won't be a rest. The more I can cover, the better it will be. That's what I call a rest.[19]

President de Valera declared that the news of the visit was 'a source of joy and pleasure'. What had originally been a visit of 'a day or two' soon expanded to three. Arrangements had to be made. Kennedy took a crash course in Irish history, secured the battle flag of the Civil War Irish Brigade to present and studied the writings of

Irish poets. Dave Powers commented, 'He's getting so Irish, the next thing we know he'll be talking with a brogue.' When Powers told him that the Gaelic Cinneide could be translated as 'helmet head', Kennedy commented, 'Let's keep that quiet.' State Department information officers were called in. One of them commented,

> Here we are briefing this man, giving him everything we've got on Ireland, trying to forestall every query he might have, and knowing all the time he probably has ten times as much information on Ireland as we'll ever have at his fingers' ends.

Pierre Salinger told a group of Irish journalists, 'I guarantee that the President will surprise you guys with his knowledge of Irish history.' Kennedy would have no need for his album of Irish music, a constant companion on other trips.[20]

Kennedy and Kiernan quickly put together plans for the establishment of an America Ireland Foundation to foster cultural and educational exchanges and joint research projects. The proposal had been first made by Kiernan in a 1962 St. Patrick's Day speech in Boston. The foundation was incorporated on the eve of the trip.[21]

Pierre Salinger and O'Donnell went to Ireland to coordinate plans for what Salinger declared to be the most important visit to Ireland 'since that of St. Patrick'. Drafts of speeches were prepared by T. P. O'Neill of the National Library of Ireland and Arthur Cheslaw of the US Embassy.[22] Then there was the matter of the entourage. Just about every White House staffer and other officials of Irish extraction, 50 in all, went directly to Ireland on a presidential plane. Expecting her third child, Jackie did not go, but two of the Kennedy sisters, Eunice Shriver and Jean Smith, did. All Irish relatives were alerted.

Kennedy's itinerary originally included visits to Dublin, Wexford, Cork and Galway, but he agreed to the last minute addition of Limerick. What about Northern Ireland? Terence O'Neill, the Prime Minister of Northern Ireland, in early May invited Kennedy to open a public park that encompassed the Giant's Causeway along the Antrim coast; it could all be done in a mere three hours. O'Neill later said that he saw this suggestion as something of an ecumenical gesture, but there was to be no stopover in the sectarian statelet. Kennedy informed him that he 'was genuinely sorry that my schedule simply leaves me no room for this stop in June'. Letting him down easy, Kennedy concluded, 'The next time you are in Washington, we can meet and have a talk.' O'Neill did not forget and he arranged to be in Washington in September, but Kennedy's schedule remained filled to the brim. O'Neill said that 'everyone was disappointed' about this. A consolation prize was at hand — lunch with Robert Kennedy (from which Bobby bolted on more important business). At length O'Neill concluded that he had been kept away from the grand photo opportunity at the White House because of the pending scheduled visit of An Taoiseach, Sean F. Lemass (*Document 12*).[23]

In Ireland interest and then excitement mounted. By the eve of the President's arrival the newspapers were plastered with special feature stories. One journal declared, 'The trickle of Kennedy material that began in the national press as soon as the visit became official had turned into a spate' by late June. Ambassador McCloskey and Irish Foreign Affairs officials descended on Wexford to take charge of arrangements. Orders were issued. The stage had to be moved. The quay was being scrapped and a huge pile of debris accumulated. McCloskey wanted to know what they intended to do about this. Andrew J. Minihan, Chairman of the Urban District Council, otherwise mayor, had had enough: 'What we were doing is that we were bringing about another hundred loads and adding to it so when the President came he thought he was in the Alps.' Kennedy was hugely amused by the report that Minihan had said that if the President wanted chrome, 'he can find it on Madison Avenue'. At the Kennedy homestead at Dunganstown, Mrs. Ryan took charge of arrangements. One relative appeared at a planning session who hadn't visited in 20 years. Mrs. Ryan objected to his inclusion. His name — John Kennedy! Despite family protests, the farmyard got a quick resurfacing. [24]

Jerry Bruno, a Kennedy advance man, arrived first: 'The feeling in Dublin was unreal. People were literally talking about Kennedy's visit in the streets, in a pub where I stopped for a beer, everywhere. When I mentioned to someone that I worked for John Kennedy, the whole place went into an uproar.' When journalist Frank D'Arcy heard Kennedy on the radio declaring that he was looking forward to visiting the land of the Kennedys and the Fitzgeralds, but also of the Hickeys and the Hannons, D'Arcy knew the visit would be a great occasion. A columnist in the *Irish Independent* declared: 'The flags are flying, the banners are bellowing, the freedom scrolls are adorned, the Dáil chamber ready for its august guest and the country is waiting to clutch him to its heart.'[25]

First came Germany and Kennedy's stirring 'Ich bin ein Berliner' speech. As he flew to Ireland he reminisced about his 1947 visit. He told O'Donnell of the English lady who drove with him to Wexford: and how he had felt like kicking her out of the car. When O'Donnell said to him that this time 'you won't be mixed up with any members of the British nobility', Kennedy replied, 'Good'.[26]

Chapter Three

COMING BACK

There was drama in the air as the huge presidential
jet roared down the runway at Dublin airport on the
evening of 26 June 1963, and Irish people do not squan-
der dramatic situations. What unfolded was something
like a dream come true for generations of Irish people,
at home and abroad. A representative of the Great
Famine emigration had reached the top in America and
he would be in Ireland — for four days. John F. Kennedy,
President of the United States of America, was coming
from a tumultuous visit to Germany, with the people of
Europe and elsewhere watching on television. Ireland
was in the spotlight.

Kennedy's visit came at the best of times, for Ireland
was in the midst of an economic boom — the first period
of sustained industrial development since the country
gained independence. This achievement was due sub-
stantially to the vision, determination and intelligence of
Sean Francis Lemass, An Taoiseach and the economic
Abraham Lincoln of his country. As well, Ireland had
also attained a prominent role in international affairs
through its active involvement in the United Nations.
A peacekeeping mission in the Congo, in which some
Irish troops were killed. And Fredrick Boland, President
of the General Assembly, was hammering down Nikita
Khrushchev.

From 26 June to the 29th, Kennedy did everything in Ireland except kiss the Blarney Stone and climb Croagh Patrick.

At the official greetings at the airport, An Uachtaráin na hÉireann, the elderly Eamon de Valera, the world's senior freedom fighter, greeted his young colleague first in the Irish language and then in English. Dev had been host to his father exactly 25 years before. There was a guard of honour composed of Congo veterans. Evelyn Lincoln noted that Kennedy appeared relaxed and happy, 'all the cares of the world had suddenly gone from his shoulders'.[1]

This was followed by an open motorcade into the city. According to the critical Thomas Kiernan, the crowds were small and restrained. Brian Inglis observed the same thing. Perhaps people were trying to get the measure of the man, waiting to see how he wanted them to respond to him. Kenny O'Donnell had a different recollection. He remembered, 'The whole noisy city was bursting with Gaelic pride' and 'everybody seemed to have tears in their eyes'. The correspondent of the *Cork Examiner* saw it the same way: 'He came to the land of his forebears amid a greeting of such pride, such tumult and such heart-gripping warmth as Ireland has never known.' Newspaper photographs showed a jammed O'Connell Street. As his motorcade entered the city centre Kennedy stood up in his convertible. It passed through de Valera's mind, 'what an easy target he would have been', but thought, 'there was no danger about it at all'.[2]

After a stop at the President's mansion, Kennedy went across the Phoenix Park to the residence of the US Ambassador. After looking over the place, Kennedy told McCloskey: 'Matt, this is better than the White House.' He shortly announced that he would support any

Democratic presidential candidate in 1968 who would
agree to appoint him Ambassador to Ireland.[3]

The next morning Kennedy was up early and eager to
go to Wexford. After a meeting with Sean Lemass, the
presidential party flew by helicopter to the port town of
New Ross, on the River Barrow, from where his people
had emigrated. On the way down Kennedy had the pilot
circle around Lismore castle. Near the landing site a
hundred children in white pullovers were arranged to
spell out 'fáilte' ('welcome'); thereafter they were known
as the fáilte kids. As the Kennedy party entered the town,
all plans were swept aside. Andrew Minihan:

> Immediately his car arrived he jumped out of the
> car and he went straight forward to me and said:
> "Mayor Minihan," said he, "my brother Ted sends
> you his kindest regards and he said he had a whale
> of a time with you here in New Ross." And I knew
> from that minute that I was speaking to a man.

A Secret Service agent having cut the cable, the public
address system was not working. Minihan declared: 'Now
I know we are in trouble.' Everyone, including Kennedy
laughed, and relaxed. After a welcoming address,
Minihan presented Kennedy with a small piece of stone
from the Giant's Causeway, with the remark: 'If the
President couldn't go to the Giant's Causeway, the Giant's
Causeway should go to the President.' Kennedy laughed
again. He led a chorus of children in singing *Kelly, the Boy
from Killane*. The American Embassy had instructed local
officials not to let people shake hands with him because
of his bad back, but Kennedy would have none of this.
'He went around amongst the people and everybody was
absolutely thrilled by him,' Dorothy Tubridy observed.
'The minute he decided to go among them. they nearly

went wild with excitement.' For the rest of the visit the nation was galvanised.[4]

Then it was up the road to the townland of Dunganstown and the Kennedy homestead. Jack and his sisters were greeted by Mary Ryan and her family, with cousins coming from miles around (presumably including John Kennedy). What Brian Inglis observed was a gathering of kin who were 'self-possessed, neither over-awed nor over-pleased with themselves — a decent family taking the whole thing calmly and sensibly'. Mary Ryan said, 'Cousin Jack came here like an ordinary member of the family. He crouched at the fire and blew the bellows. He asked everything about the family and the farm.' Jim Kennedy observed that Jack remembered every detail of his last visit, including the layout of the farm. After tea and sandwiches, the American president was given a large white wool blanket 'made from sheep right here' and a blackthorn walking stick, a bit of china for his wife, a handkerchief for Caroline and a hand-carved boat 'for the little boy'. He was shown the photographs he had sent the family of his 1947 visit and he planted a tree. To Mrs. Ryan he said: 'I promise you I won't come more than once every ten years to cause you this trouble again.' His parting words were: 'Cousin Mary, the next time I come I'll bring Jackie and the children.' The *Irish Times* story of the visit was headlined, *Cousin Jack Comes to See the Folks*. A simple, natural occasion, yet eloquent for that.

Kennedy then went to Wexford town to lay a wreath at a statue of John Barry, native son and father of the American navy. Again he joined a chorus of children in singing, this time his favourite Irish song, *The Boys of Wexford*.

The presidential party returned that afternoon to Dublin for a lively, somewhat disorderly garden party of

1,500 people on the grounds of Aras an Uachtaráin. 'Even that,' noted Inglis,' gave the Irish some satisfaction, as they read of the social climbers vainly jostling each other for a glimpse of JFK.'[5]

On Friday morning, 28 June, Kennedy flew to Cork and another tumultuous reception. As he drove into the city, he pointed to a sign held by one of the welcomers: 'JFK and Dev, for Boston and New York — but the boys who beat the Black and Tans were the boys from County Cork.' In his speech he extolled Ireland, which he said 'was the first country to lead what was the most powerful tide in the twentieth century, the desire for national independence, the desire to be free . . .'. As he did in his Dáil address, he pointed to a new mission for Ireland: 'To lead the free world, to join with other countries in the free world, to do in the 1960s what Ireland did in the early part of this century and indeed has done for the last 800 years, and that is associate itself intimately with the principles of freedom' (*See Document 16*).

He introduced Dave Powers and Larry O'Brien, who were seated with their Irish relations, as well as Monsignor Michael O'Mahony: 'The pastor at the church I go to, who comes from Cork. He is the pastor of a poor, humble flock in Palm Beach, Florida.' Not everyone was in good humour. He encountered some of his Fitzgerald cousins who declared that they 'were tired of hearing about the Kennedys of New Ross'. Kennedy explained to them that his grandfather would claim his county of origin was that of the person to whom he was speaking. The *Cork Examiner* (29 June) responded to the event: 'His display of uninhibited friendliness could not hide the fact that behind it stood one of the great men of the world. His hosts, and all were his hosts on this occasion, appreciated the distinction and loved him all the more for his modesty.'

Then it was back to Dublin and a visit to Arbour Hill, where the leaders of the 1916 rebellion are buried. To Kennedy the drill performed by the Irish Army cadets was a highlight of his visit. They were to perform at his funeral five months later. His sisters Eunice and Jean visited two special schools — in Blackrock and Knockmaroon, both of which were receiving financial aid from the Kennedy Foundation.[6]

Then there was Kennedy's address to the Oireachtas, the Irish parliament, the Dáil and the Seanad (Senate). This was the first occasion that a visiting statesman had addressed the two bodies, and that any proceedings had been televised. He honoured the occasion, and the Irish people, with a full, formal and serious speech of 26 minutes; vintage Kennedy, complete with literary allusions and stirring words. He began by presenting the Irish Government with the American Civil War battle flag of the 69th Division of the Irish Brigade, of which it has been said was 'probably the most illustrious standard which Irish exiled soldiers carried on any continent'. Speaking of the great flow of Irish emigrants to America, he recalled that James Joyce had described the Atlantic Ocean as a 'bitter bowl of tears'.

He gave considerable attention to the long Irish struggle for national freedom, quoting the words of Henry Grattan: 'A country enlightened as Ireland, chartered as Ireland, armed as Ireland and injured as Ireland, will be satisfied with nothing less than liberty.' This bitter effort was of world significance: 'Those who suffer beyond that wall I saw in Berlin on Wednesday need not despair for the future. Let them remember the constancy, the faith, the endurance and the ultimate success of the Irish.' After a roar of approval, he continued: 'Let them remember as I did yesterday, the boys of Wexford who fought with heart and hand, to burst in twain the galling chain and free their native land.'

He also spoke with admiration of Ireland's economic and social progress, noting that the process was not completed. He praised the Irish state's role in international affairs. Ireland was 'an example and standard for other small nations'; it was 'an example and inspiration' for nations seeking national freedom. He concluded: 'My friends, Ireland's hour has come. You have something to give to the world, and that is a future of peace with freedom' (*See Document 17*).

One observer seated in the back of the gallery looked down across a sea of bald heads and observed the contrast between the young, dynamic American president and the aged, if vigorous, Irish parliamentarians. Brian Inglis noted that 'towards the end of his speech his audience was visibly affected; hardened politicians wept in their seats.' 'What was most welcomed about the speech, and the whole visit', Inglis declared, 'was that the President treated his hosts as adults — something his compatriots, and English journalists, find hard to do.' Sean O Luing, a Dáil official, saw the general response in the chamber as being, 'At last, we have arrived!' The *Cork Examiner* declared that Kennedy 'spoke with intense feeling, with manifest conviction, and with such wisdom that the case and cause of Ireland were put into clearer perspective than could be within the capacity of any of our countrymen.' What Kennedy had not mentioned was partition, the major political issue. Rather than address this contentious matter, he directed all of his attention to the positive developments achieved by the Irish nation.[7]

After receiving honorary degrees from both the University of Dublin (Trinity College) and the National University of Ireland at a Dublin Castle ceremony,

Kennedy joined de Valera, Lemass and other Irish leaders for a dinner party. He asked de Valera about his experiences in 1916. De Valera told him: 'There were many times when the key in my jail cell door was turned and I thought that my time had come.' But there was more than recollections that night. They talked about Irish nationalism, partition and the Irish language. Based on the discussion, de Valera later sent Kennedy a copy of Arthur Griffith's book on the course for Irish nationhood, *The Resurrection of Hungary* (*See Document 19*). Kennedy saw the emphasis on the restoration of the Irish language as an impediment to raising Irish educational standards, while Lemass and de Valera provided their rationalisation of the need to revive the language. Lemass also noted Kennedy's intense interest about the places through which he travelled. Always there were questions, questions.[8]

On his last day in Ireland, Kennedy addressed huge gatherings in Galway and Limerick. Before a packed crowd at Limerick racecourse, Mrs. Frances Condell, the Lady Mayoress, provided an introduction, filled with wit and insight, that in its length bordered on presumption. Kennedy whispered to Ken O'Donnell: 'These introductions would seem awfully long if they weren't such good speakers.' He publicly hailed Mrs. Condell's statement as 'the best speech I have heard in Europe.' Then to Shannon for his departure. Flying there he said to Ken O'Donnell: 'I wish I could stay here for another week, or a month.' Larry O'Brien observed, 'The visit deeply moved him and rekindled in him a sense of his Irish heritage' (*See Documents 18, 19*).

At the airport, rather than say he was flying to England, Kennedy said he was 'going to another country'; everyone laughed. But this was no ordinary send-off. Citing the words of the poem spoken to him by Mrs. de Valera, Kennedy told the crowd he would 'come back in the Springtime' to see 'old Shannon's face once again'. With the Bunratty chorus singing *Come back to Erin*, the President of the United States took his leave.[9]

The organisers of the departure ceremony could not have created an atmosphere of emotion without it being in the hearts and minds of the participants. Kennedy obviously was moved by it all. It was a unique occasion to cap an extraordinary four days. Only the visit of a Pope would equal if not exceed it.

The Kennedy visit had spanned four days. But it was a full affair; any more would have been too much. A writer in the *Irish Times* referred to the tour as 'the hurricane visit', adding that Kennedy was able 'to show Ireland to the Irish in a way that they themselves had never seen it and he also introduced Ireland to the world as a modern go-ahead nation.' An editorial in the *Irish Independent* declared that 'the visit fulfilled the highest hopes' and that 'it was difficult to say whom seemed more pleased, the guest or the host'. The *Irish Press* commented, 'Here is a man with the gift of happiness.' *Hibernia*, a weekly journal, was relieved that the visit had gone so well: 'It seems certain that the responsible tone taken up by the Irish papers and Telefis Éireann (Irish Television) succeeded in dissuading most of the foreign correspondents from filing stories loaded with shamrock and bathed in Celtic eyewash.'

This was not the view of the Earl of Arran. Writing in the London *Evening News*, in the best tradition of grumpy English popular journalism, he referred to 'the boggy, slushy, poteen-ridden atmosphere' during the visit, which made him anxious about Kennedy's 'true feelings for Britain'. A letter to the *Irish Times* took exception to the disorder at the garden party, declaring, 'It is these ignorant hooligans — men and women — who let down all decent Irish folk'. The general opinion in Ireland, however, was that the whole occasion had gone very well.[10]

The London *Sunday Telegraph* (30 June) put the visit in the broadest Anglo-Irish perspective:

> Whoever writes the ultimate great work on the decline and fall of the British Empire must pay particular attention to Ireland. It could be argued that it was the southern Irish who broke Britain's will to rule; forced her to adopt self-government as the goal of colonial policy; taught the inevitability of successful resistance and the probability that old enemies could become firm friends.

Foreign press coverage of the visit was almost entirely positive and favourable. *Time* magazine, in its issue of 12 July, had a cover story on Lemass and the Irish economic revival, *Lifting the Green Curtain*. This was exactly the kind of attention needed by a country in the throes of development. This was the first and only time that an Irish political figure appeared on the cover of this important American publication.

Ambassador Kiernan later declared what he saw as the significance of the affair: 'I think his coming back to Ireland was a closing of a chapter that began with the famine' of the late 1840s. After decades of despair and failure,

> here was a success at top level. Here was a fellow who came from famine stock on both paternal and maternal sides and who had reached the very top in the United States. That was felt throughout the country. I think in that sense you could say he wasn't coming back as the king; he was coming at the end

of a bad epoch, a bad century. And whether he felt it
or not, I don't know, because in his speeches he did
refer to it so much, kept referring to that period... as
if it was yesterday, which is very much the Irish way
of talking.[11]

Many people in Ireland naturally wanted to know what
went on in the discussions of Kennedy, de Valera and
Lemass. Speaking in Dáil Éireann on 3 July, Lemass said
that the matter of partition had been raised — but in the
context of an examination of world affairs, and no proposals for action had been presented. There would be
opportunity for further talks as Kennedy had invited
Lemass to make a state visit to the US.[12]

Before the visit Kennedy was well aware of his Irish
heritage and carefully prepared himself for the event,
but it was apparent that as a result of this experience,
indeed during the course of it, he experienced a strengthened sense of this identity. Dave Powers noted that the
President seemed to become more and more Irish as
the visit continued. Of course what politician, or anyone
else for that matter, would not be swept along by the
enthusiasm, hospitality and abundant goodwill that he
encountered. But this renewed sense of being did not
evaporate when he left.[13]

Chapter Four

AFTER

Kennedy did not return immediately to the United States, but went to that other country. After meeting with Harold Macmillan, he went with his sisters to visit the grave of Kathleen Kennedy Hartington. Then he was off to a three-day visit to Italy and a visit with the new Pope, John Paul I. More cheering crowds, and finally back to the US.

Upon his return to Washington, he was gently needled by his potential rival and friend, Senator Barry Goldwater, who noted that the affairs of state had been left aside while the President visited his 'native Ireland'. The bulk of the presidential entourage had returned directly to Washington and Drew Pearson, a noted columnist, published a list of the participants on the junket and condemned the trip as a waste of the taxpayers' money. As far as Larry O'Brien was concerned, 'that was one column nobody in the White House gave a damn about'.[1]

Kennedy told several people, including Jackie, that his time in Ireland had been the happiest days of his life. He showed the films of the visit over and over again, finally being reduced to an audience of one. Although he had told Sean Lemass that he thought the effort to use the educational system to revive the Irish language was a misuse of valuable resources, he now seemed interested in Gaelic. Paul Fay noted that after the Irish visit, Kennedy could not pass by Ted Kennedy's Irish-speaking nanny without a greeting in Irish. 'If he thought he was not pronouncing his phrases correctly', he would get her assistance and 'then off he would go wishing "Cead Mile Failte" with a sure touch . . . '. He mentioned to his wife that he would like some buttons of the Irish Brigade for his blazer. Jackie inquired of his military aide if the 'Wild Geese' regiment still existed; if it did not, would the general then get Irish Army buttons.[2]

Shortly after his return he wrote to Sinead de Valera to thank her for her insights into Irish literature and more: 'I hope you will not dismiss these words as mere flattery, as a wise old Irish lady once told me — "A kind word never broke a tooth".' When Kennedy was mobbed at a public gathering at the end of July, President de Valera wrote to him, 'I was somewhat relieved to see by the newspapers that you are being mobbed in the White House gardens as you were here.' He also sent along a copy of Arthur Griffith's book, *The Resurrection of Hungary*, in which Griffith outlined the methods of non-violent agitation and obstruction which were later employed in Ireland to achieve self-government. Kennedy replied, 'I appreciate your thought more than I can say and I shall take it with me this weekend.'[3]

The Irish Government had presented Kennedy with a gift of a treaty made by the O'Kennedy clan and an Anglo-Irish family in the thirteenth century; he put this in the Oval Office. Lemass noted that the President was very interested in the fact that the Kennedys were powers in the land long ago. The Kennedy party also had been given a variety of gifts by public bodies and individuals, including a bottle of Knock holy water, articles of clothing and various utensils, but also some animals. The President very much wanted the animals, but with no publicity.

An Irish wolfhound puppy, arrived by arrangement as did a Connemara donkey and an Irish deer. The dog was delivered just after the death of his infant son, Patrick. Kennedy wrote to its donor, Father Thomas Kennedy of Rosenallis, County Laois, 'It arrived at a time when it was most helpful. It helped to ease our feelings during a very difficult time.' He also was keen to get more copies of *The Boys of Wexford*. The Irish Ambassador saw to this matter. His sister Eunice asked Sean Lemass to send her a recording of the song to give her brother as a Christmas present.[4]

The matter of Ireland and the Irish connection was not lost in the ensuing affairs of government and politics. When a group of Irish teachers visited the White House in August they were given 'a special and leisurely visit' with Kennedy. Upon his request, they sang an Irish song for him, *Sailing for the Low Lands Low*. Also, Kennedy had invited Sean Lemass to visit the United States in October. Responding to the hospitality shown him in Ireland, the President took exceptional interest in the preparations for the event.

The State Department responded by asking Dr. Kiernan what Ireland was looking for out of the visit:

> The State Department were asking me, accustomed as they are to "beg and bum" nations thrumming around, "What were we going to ask for — what proposal were we going to put forward?" And we couldn't believe it. We didn't come for any proposal.

The failure to ask for something became a grievance with the US diplomats: 'The attitude and feeling was that something should have been asked.' It was Kennedy himself who came up with something — joint maritime research, with the costs to be borne by the United States.

The idea for this undoubtedly was stimulated by Brendan O'Kelly, Chairman of the Irish Fisheries Board, who had taken it upon himself to write to Kennedy and suggest such a scheme.[5]

Lemass was in the US from 11 to 20 October, during which time he went on a rigorous tour of Boston, New York, Philadelphia and Chicago. Kennedy informed de Valera that he told Lemass: 'The schedule was fit only for a veteran campaigner, but that I was sure he would survive it as I survived my trip to Ireland.' Kennedy provided every possible amenity to the Lemass party. It travelled by presidential jet. Then there was Washington where he spent three days. Kennedy arranged elaborate welcoming ceremonies, including a 40-minute motorcade around the centre of the capital, complete with flags, decorations and a street-spanning banner. Special badges were provided (green background, golden harp); Kennedy wore one. He also arranged for a film of the Lemass visit be made and given to him.

Lemass had the opportunity for further discussions with Kennedy, which apparently centred on Ireland's economic development programme and the imbalance in Irish-American trade. According to Ambassador Kiernan, Lemass got along 'amazingly well' with Kennedy, although the Prime Minister did dwell on a 'lot of statistical data'. Kennedy later told de Valera that he was 'most impressed' by the development programme. Lemass noted that when he first met Kennedy he was struck by Kennedy's keen interest in Ireland and the Irish, but now he observed that Kennedy was interested in just about everything. The O'Kennedy treaty was in the Oval Office and Kennedy played the film of his Irish visit over and over.[6]

The state dinner in honour of the visiting head of government had the unusual feature of Irish music by the Air Force bagpipe band. Afterwards, Kennedy, Lemass, the pipers and a dozen friends went upstairs for a party. Ted Kennedy sang and Gene Kelly sang and danced. According to Jim Reed, who was there, 'the President was just overcome with it all'. Reed noted that during the singing of the Irish songs, 'the President had the sweetest and saddest kind of look on his face. He was standing by himself, leaning against the doorway, and just seemed transported into a world of imagination.'[7]

Kennedy presented Lemass with a set of hand-made golf clubs, declaring that he looked forward to a game with him. He sent along for President de Valera, a replica of a sword of George Washington's, an appropriate gift 'in view of the large number of men from Ireland who bore arms in defence of the United States in our Revolutionary Wars and in succeeding conflicts.' He also told de Valera, 'I want you to know of the particular pride and pleasure that the Prime Minister's visit afforded me.'[8]

The events of 22 November 1963 are well known. The day before, Kennedy spoke at San Antonio, Texas, during which he referred to the story of Frank O'Connor, the masterful Irish short-story writer:

> Frank O'Connor tells us in one of his books how, as a boy, he and his friends would make their way across the countryside, and when they came to an orchard wall that seemed too high and too doubtful to try and too difficult to permit their voyage to continue, they took off their hats and tossed them over the wall — and then they had no choice but to follow them. This nation has tossed its cap over the wall of space, and we have no choice but to follow it.

Ken O'Donnell thought to himself, 'Only Kennedy would be telling an Irish story by an Irish writer in Texas.'[9]

Returning to Washington on that day, Jacqueline Kennedy told Dave Powers and Kenny O'Donnell how she wished she had been with them in Ireland with Jack, as he told her that those were the happiest days of his life. She also requested that the Irish honour guard, that had so impressed him at Arbour Hill in Dublin, attend his funeral. Later, in his honour, the army cadet unit adopted a flag of the colours and crests of the Fitzgeralds and the Kennedys. Representing the Dunganstown Kennedys was Mary Ryan, a daughter of Mrs. Ryan, who was flown to Washington as a guest of the US Government. Jackie gave her the rosary beads Kennedy had in his pocket and one of his Navy identification tags for her mother. The following St. Patrick's Day she put shamrock on the grave of her husband.[10]

There were many tributes to the dead President, with some of the most notable being provided by two of the great men of Irish literature. Playwright Sean O'Casey declared: 'Peace, who was becoming bright-eyed, now sits in the shadow of death; her handsome champion has been killed as he walked by her very side. Her gallant boy is dead. What a cruel, foul and most unnatural murder!' Frank O'Connor, master of the short story, commented: 'John Fitzgerald Kennedy was a miracle, in three different ways he broke through age-old American prejudices — against Catholics, against Irishmen and against intellectuals' (*See Document 22*).

The reaction in Ireland was extraordinary and almost disturbing. Sean Lemass announced that the Government would provide a state monument for Kennedy. Later he said that the planned national concert hall would be named in Kennedy's honour. This was never built, but when another building was remodelled into a concert hall it was simply named the National Concert Hall. At one point there was a proposal to rename Westmoreland Street in the centre of Dublin, but this was not done. A few minor streets around the country were named in his honour. Irish people shed many tears when Kennedy died, but only in the New Ross town hall is there a bust of him, although this is not mentioned in the town tourist booklet. The flag of the Irish Brigade he presented is displayed in a case on a stair landing in Leinster House. At Shannon airport there is a painting depicting his departure. A marker in Eyre Square, Galway notes the occasion of his speech.[11] A national arboretum and forest in Wexford, opened in 1968, bears his name.[12]

The Kennedy homestead remains in the ownership of the Ryan family, although thousands of tourists annually make their way down the narrow, winding road to see it. Until 1993 only a small wooden sign marked the cottage, of which one room is open to the public. Over the years, the crowds became a burden to the Ryan family. In Northern Ireland the homesteads of the forebears of American presidents have been restored and made into public monuments. If the politicians in Dublin have been indifferent to this matter, it is a wonder that Wexford County Council has not done something, perhaps widening the road, building a small car park or providing a suitable historical marker.

Despite the lack of official commemoration, John F. Kennedy received the highest accolade given by Irish people: his picture was put on the wall beside that of good Pope John XXIII in many a home.[13]

This was not the end of the association of the Kennedys with Ireland. Jacqueline Kennedy and her children spent six weeks there the summer of 1967. When she arrived at Shannon airport, she declared; 'I am so happy to be here in this land my husband loved so much.' Staying

at a home in Woodstown, County Waterford, she visited
Dunganstown, attended a state dinner in Dublin Castle,
watched the Irish Derby at the Curragh and saw a play.
The children spent a day at the Ryan farm. The Ryans
later visited Jackie in New York.[14]

Ted Kennedy visited Ireland in 1964, and several times
subsequently. He was the Kennedy to witness the eruption
of the nationalist/Catholic population of Northern
Ireland. He took a strong interest in this development. In
1971 he urged the British Government to withdraw from
Northern Ireland. He joined with a group of Irish-
American political leaders, in the 'Friends of Ireland', to
oppose American contributions to the Irish Republican
Army while, at the same time, urging the British Government to seek an agreed political solution. Kennedy has
maintained this active position through to the Clinton
Administration.[15]

Robert Kennedy only visited Ireland once — in 1949,
although he had planned to do so again at the end of
May 1968 for the dedication of a memorial to his brother,
apparently in Wexford. The visit was precluded by his
campaign for the Democratic nomination for president.
In his study of Irish-American political culture, Edward
Levine declared that in his personal characteristics —
his loyalty, pugnacity, concern for others — Bobby 'was
far more the Irish politician' than his older brother.
Others shared this opinion.[16]

The late President's son, John F. Jr., has shown some
interest in his Irish heritage. He played the part of an
Irishman in an amateur theatrical production in New
York and has made a couple of quiet, private visits to
Ireland.[17]

The Kennedy of the new generation who has taken the
greatest interest in Ireland is Bobby's son, Joseph Patrick

Kennedy II, congressman from the family district in Massachusetts since 1987. Joe Kennedy has been outspoken in his assertion that it was time Britain left the six counties. He has carried his efforts to Belfast, with attendant media attention. Among his other actions was to insert an amendment to defence legislation, requiring foreign defence contractors to adhere to American equal opportunity laws (this action aimed at Shorts aircraft company in Belfast) and to introduce a resolution that the President appoint a special US peace envoy to Northern Ireland. This proposal was incorporated in the 1992 Democratic Party platform. He had also served as co-chairman, with Mayor Raymond Flynn of Boston, of Northern Ireland Justice Watch, a body that has monitored the process of criminal justice in the six counties.[18]

Then, on 17 March 1993, President Clinton nominated Jean Kennedy Smith as Ambassador to Ireland. Mrs. Smith, of course, had been with the President in 1963 and had returned several times since. She arrived in Ireland in time for the thirteenth anniversary of her brother's visit as President of the United States of America.[19]

This renewed Kennedy link with Ireland came at a time when the community of New Ross has finally decided to do something about the Kennedy connection. In 1988, a Kennedy Trust was established to promote the cultural, economic and environmental development of the town. With the support of a group of Irish patrons, the Kennedy family, Bord Fáilte and the Irish Government, the Trust began to act.

Sean Reidy was appointed manager, a small office was opened in the town tourist centre and a couple of computers containing genealogical information were installed. In 1993 the Trust unveiled an ambitious three million pounds programme, which would include a Kennedy

museum, art gallery and lecture hall in two adjourning
abandoned warehouses along the quay from which John
F. Kennedy spoke. In front of the centre the Trust pro-
poses to moor a full-scale replica of an 1840s emigrant
ship. Moreover, the Viking, Norman and medieval history
of the community would be brought into focus. This
would make New Ross a complement to the nearby
heritage park at Ferrycarrig, which contains replicas of
habitations from pre-historic times to 700 AD. Although a
fund-raising campaign is planned for the United States,
the full development of the plan is dependant on very
substantial EC funding. Caroline Kennedy Schlossberg
and her husband Edwin have taken a strong interest in
the project.

Chapter Five

LOOKING BACK

Thirty years later John F. Kennedy and his times remain of great interest to many people. Some of the interest is due to various accounts of his personal life; and, some people have argued that, after all, he was overrated as a political leader. The scandal-mongers will probably go on for a long time yet, but it is likely that the efforts of the revisionists, begrudgers and their like have reached their apogee and now there appears to be a swing back to clarity and perspective.

A common refrain among some critics, which has achieved considerable public acceptance, is that Kennedy was not very important, after all, because he was not a particularly successful president. They declare that he failed to get most of his proposals through Congress. Obviously based on the principle that getting ideas into the political pipeline is the first step towards legislative achievement, Kennedy submitted more than a thousand proposals. Of the 53 major proposals he presented to the 87th Congress, 33 became law; of the 54 he submitted to the next session, 40 were passed, and of the 58 he sent forward in his last year, 35 became law. Theodore White declared that the Kennedy presidency encompassed 'the most vigorous three years of legislation since the first term of Roosevelt'.

On the other hand, there were major proposals that he was not able to get through. John W. McCormack, House Speaker at the time, has pointed out that the Kennedy Administration had a four-year program. Support for these bills was gaining strength and an election year was coming up. By almost any assessment the scenario for 1964 was that Kennedy would have achieved re-election by a substantial margin, carrying with him many new Democratic members of Congress. Thus, he would have had a strong mandate, and this legislation would have passed, as it did under President Johnson. As well, there is more to being an effective head of the executive branch than simply pushing through legislation.

During his presidency significant progress was made in many areas of national concern. The economy was strong, with low inflation, high employment and rising living standards. After a period of prolonged difficulty, it was clear that all Americans would enjoy their civil rights, and that segregation and blatant discrimination would be abolished. Increased national expenditures for education and social welfare were in the works.[1]

Of great importance was the evolving relationship with the Soviet Union. Having avoided military conflict in the Cuban missile crisis, the two superpowers were becoming conciliatory. The nuclear test ban agreement of June 1963 is clear evidence of this new situation.

What about the US involvement in Vietnam? Kennedy recognised Vietnam as a quagmire in which he did not intend to be caught. There is persuasive evidence that he planned to end the US presence there after his re-election in 1964. He stated this privately to some of his closest associates — Charles Bartlett, Kenneth O'Donnell, Mike Mansfield and Roger Hilsman. He did not indicate his intention to Dean Rusk and other officials, but they were only functionaries. In October 1963 he made the symbolic gesture of ordering the return of 5,000 troops, specifically including helicopter pilots. He warned his staff to be prepared, that full withdrawal could easily make him the most unpopular president in American history. James D. Barber believes that 'a saving sense of proportion' would have prevented Kennedy from taking the plunge in Vietnam.[2]

Much of what has been written about Kennedy in one way or another deals with his personality and character. What this study has been concerned with is his self-image, particularly his sense of Irish identity.

One of his most severe contemporary critics was Murray Kempton, a columnist for the *New York Post* and later for the *Spectator*, an English periodical. In an article at the end of the 1960 campaign, Kempton declared that Kennedy disdained his Irish background. To Kempton, he was a 'changeling': 'In point of fact the name could be Cabot or Bradford or Saltonstall.' Looking at the array of Democratic candidates on the platform in Boston Garden on election eve, Kempton declared: 'The Massachusetts ticket is all Irish; its members have the cold eyes and slack faces of IRA members who have gone into another line of work.' It was Kempton's impression that Kennedy spoke briefly and then left 'as fast as he could . . . purging his trousers of the Boston Irish'.[3]

Kennedy was not running away from anyone. Although his speech to the packed Garden was short, it was also forceful and eloquent. Moreover, he had to be on time for his final national television appearance nearby and a cheering mass of people stood in-between. Indeed, Kennedy did not have to have a mass meeting in Boston; he already had wrapped up all the votes he would be getting in his home region. He was simply paying homage to the people who had supported him on the way up (although he rightly suspected he should have spent the last couple of days in California). The bunch of politicians on the stage might not have been an impressive lot to someone like Kempton, but they had backed Jack all the way for the presidency, many of them working in various parts of the country. For example, Thomas P. 'Tip' O'Neill worked in the campaign in Missouri. Although Kennedy had enjoyed many advantages that they had not, he knew them, liked them and worked with them. Even as president, he did not hesitate to ask for their assistance. On one occasion he telephoned from the White House to a Massachusetts golf course to get in touch with Patrick J. 'Sonny' McDonough, a colourful and notorious political operator. It is most unlikely that Kennedy was asking for his advice on the nuclear test ban negotiations.[4]

Kempton continued this approach during Kennedy's presidency. Since Kennedy was such an extraordinarily popular president, it would make good journalistic sense to go against the grain. He once wrote that Kennedy spoke of the Boston Irish very much the way his supposed hero, Lord Melbourne, spoke of the Irish of Dublin. Considering Kennedy's origins, Kempton declared, 'his professional aloofness from his forebears is impressive'. At the end he believed that Kennedy would like to return as John Adams to somehow elevate the Boston Irish masses. Good fare for the cranky, chauvinistic *Spectator*.[5]

There was also Malcolm Muggeridge, noted English wit and supposed debunker of pomposity. There was a nasty streak in that grinning man, and Kennedy seemed to bother him inordinately. Perhaps it was Kennedy's spirit and gusto and, I suspect, his Irish heritage. What seemed to be so offensive to Muggeridge was that Kennedy had been so successful in projecting a positive image.

Advertisement for John F. Kennedy's first newspaper article.
New York Journal American, 2 February 1941.

Photo taken by JFK in 1946 of his Dunganstown
relations. *Front row:* Kitty Kennedy, Thomas Ryan.
Middle row: Patrick Kennedy, Peggy Kennedy, Anna Kennedy,
Mary A. Ryan, Mrs Mary Kennedy Ryan, Josephine Ryan.
Back row: Mrs Kitty Kennedy, Peggy Fleming (neighbour)

Presidents Eamon de Valera and John F. Kennedy.

JFK and An Taoiseach Sean Lemass.

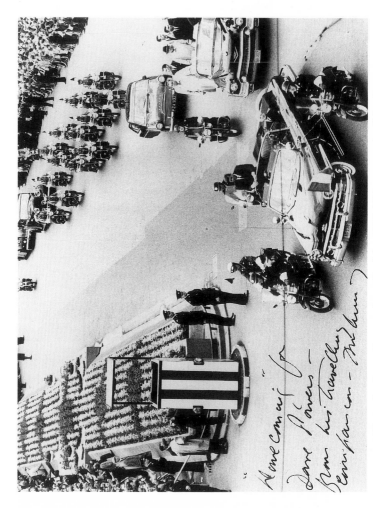

Photo by Dave Powers inscribed by JFK: "Homecoming" for Dave Powers — from his travelling companion — John Kennedy.

Dunganstown from the air during JFK visit.

Mrs. Jean Kennedy Smith, Mary Anne Ryan,
Josephine Ryan, President Kennedy, Eunice Shriver,
and Mrs. Mary Ryan in Dunganstown

Tea and cake in Dunganstown.

JFK planting a tree in Phoenix Park in Dublin.

President Kennedy addressing the Oireachtas, Dáil Éireann and Seanad Éireann.

Sean Lemass, Aileen Lemass, Sinead de Valera, President Kennedy, Eunice Shriver, President de Valera.

Jacqueline Kennedy and children visiting relations in Dunganstown. Summer 1967.

Another Englishman, Nigel Hamilton, recently has published a huge and well-researched biography, *JFK: Reckless Youth*, in which he characterises the Kennedys as upstarts. To some people in class-ridden England, this is a dismissive term, but in America getting up in the world is considered to be admirable.[6]

In a book written about Kennedy during his presidency, William Manchester declared that Kennedy had none of the mannerisms of the traditional Irish-American politician. Of course he didn't — he was of a new generation. To Manchester, this somehow made him un-Irish. He also wrote that a member of White House staff told him that the Kennedys had only a literary interest in Ireland. This sounds like Ted Sorenson, who later wrote that Kennedy had only a literary and political interest in Ireland. To have an interest and knowledge of the literature of a country is to say a lot. Unless your definition of literature is that it deals with the social intercourse and doings of the upper crust, it is about a people, their traditions and history, along with other things. Furthermore, Ted Sorenson was Kennedy's ideas man, speech writer and advisor, not his personal friend. Kennedy did not reveal himself if it did not suit him. In a later book Manchester declared that Kennedy was proud of his Irish heritage![7]

In his book *The Kennedy Imprisonment*, Garry Wills has attempted to denigrate Kennedy for being, at most, 'semi-Irish'. He cites as evidence of Kennedy's lack of feeling for his Irish heritage, the fact that he allowed one of his strategists in his first campaign to oust Grandpa Fitzgerald from the inner circle. The strategist was Joe Kane, cousin of Joe Kennedy. Hardly, an anti-Irish gesture. Furthermore, Kennedy was very happy to have Honey Fitz take him around his old bailiwicks to be introduced.[8]

Wills makes Kennedy out to be 'semi-English', citing his friendship with a few English people from his father's time in England and his appreciation of some English writers. Anyone who spent time in England likely would make friends with at least a couple of people there; anybody who speaks English can appreciate English literature. While Kennedy arranged to be greeted by cheering crowds in Paris, Berlin, Dublin, Mexico City and Rome, he did not arrange such an occasion in London. I suppose he would have got around to it.[9]

Ralph G. Martin believes that Kennedy thought like an English Whig, while William V. Shannon declared that Kennedy conducted himself like an English upper-crust politician who conferred a privilege on a constituency for having him for its absentee representative. David Burner and Thomas West assert that Kennedy was not the product of an Irish neighbourhood 'but of his father's social aspirations and an upper-class education. Moreover, he was 'something of a snob in his selection of friends.'[10]

In *John F. Kennedy and American Catholicism*, Lawrence H. Fuchs addresses this matter of ethnicity. To Fuchs, Kennedy 'symbolised exactly the opposite of many of those characteristics which were considered to be stereotypically Irish in American politics'. Fuchs compares him with other Irish-Americans who had served in Washington, including Kennedy's father, but they were of a different generation. He also says that the Irish as a whole were opposed to liberalism. If by liberalism one means a diffident preoccupation with certain principles, that is probably true. The Irish were (and are) the progressive pragmatists of American politics. Besides the pursuit of power and position, they were preoccupied with concrete, material concerns of people, like jobs, wages, housing, and working conditions. This is a difficult matter to grasp for those who are unread in the history of the American labour and urban reform movements.[11] Progressive pragmatism was Kennedy's whole political perspective, and it found considerable disfavour with liberals of the Eleanor Roosevelt and Adlai Stevenson orientation.[12]

Kennedy was a masterful professional politician and he realised it would be counter-productive to give the impression that he was preoccupied with things Irish. Thus, he presented himself differently to different people and groups. His first biographer, James McGregor Burns, later was genuinely surprised to learn that as president Kennedy travelled with an album of Irish music. 'Is this just more press-agentry?' asked Burns, only to be told that his interviewer had seen the album.[13]

The historian Donald C. Lord believed that Kennedy had a most Irish outlook. Not only did he appreciate Irish humour and fatalism, but also its idealism. He often quoted the words of George Bernard Shaw: 'Other people see things and say why. But I dream things that never were, and I say why not?' 'One such dream,' declared Lord, 'was an Irish Catholic president of the United States.'

In *Beyond the Melting Pot*, Nathan Glazer and Daniel P. Moynihan contemplated what might have been:

> Had John Fitzgerald Kennedy lived out his time he might profoundly have altered the course of the Irish-American world. Among his incomparable powers was an ability to bring together the sacred and profane streams of American public life that have somehow, for example, made foreign affairs genteel but domestic politics coarse.

They concluded that 'although he may yet emerge as the
first of a new breed, all that is certain is that we was the
last of an old one. The era of the Irish politician
culminated in Kennedy.'[14]

In his biography of Robert Kennedy, Arthur Schlesinger
has more to say about the Irish aspect than he did in his
earlier study of John Kennedy. Schlesinger refers to the
Irish-American dilemma — the clash between Irish
values and those already implanted in America. 'There
was perhaps something very Irish about it all,' he wrote,
'the loyalty to family, the irony and self-mockery, the
mingling of romantic defiance with a deep sadness;
something very Irish-American too, for the Irish legacy
in its Kennedy form had to accommodate itself to the
puritan ethic. . . .' Political careers were appropriate for
both brothers because this was an initiation 'into their
Irish legacy'. They enjoyed the folklore and jokes of
Boston politics, yet were of a new generation. 'John
Kennedy benefited indeed from the contrast. But it
remained part of their inheritance.'[15]

The people who knew him best — his family and
friends — knew of his strong Irish interest. His mother
declared, 'Jack delighted in his Irish heritage.' Red
Fay has written that Kennedy had a special feeling
for Irish people, as though he could imagine some of
them as older members of his family. Many of his long-
time close political associates, such as Dave Powers and
John E. Powers, have remarked on his love of the
stories, as well as the jokes and songs, about Boston
Irish politics. 'While Jack was a completely new type of
Irish politician,' declared Dave Powers, 'having come
from such a different background, he was, at bottom,
very Irish and he could never hear enough of the old
Irish stories.'

This sense of identity came out in other ways. When in November 1961 he met Pandit Nehru, the Indian prime minister told him about what the British had done to the Indian people; Kennedy's response was that the British had done far worse to the Irish. Dorothy Tubridy declares that Kennedy 'was very proud of his Irish heritage'; she remembers him saying that his success was due to his family and this legacy. If anyone would know what it was to feel and respond in an Irish manner, and who would spot anything false or contrived about it, it would be the residents of Ireland, and they had no difficulty in accepting him as one of their own.[16]

Kennedy was the fulfilment of Irish aspiration in American politics and government — from the battles of ward politics in the ethnic ghetto to the pinnacle of achievement in national government. And he was well aware of it. Thomas N. Brown has commented that 'the long Irish residence in the cities prepared them uniquely for a national politics shaped by the new urban America.' Furthermore, Irish-Americans have remained a powerful force in the affairs of the nation — Robert and Edward Kennedy, Eugene McCarthy, Daniel P. Moynihan, Patrick Leahy, Senators all, and three consecutive Speakers of the House of Representatives — John W. McCormack, Thomas P. O'Neill and Thomas Foley. All of them have been liberal, progressive advocates.

Irish journalists and historians have given little attention to Kennedy and his connection with their country. In a book published in 1966, journalist Tim Pat Coogan briefly celebrated the linkage between Ireland and the Irish diaspora that Kennedy represented. In his short survey of twentieth century Ireland published in 1975, John A. Murphy declared that Kennedy's success 'symbolised the endurance and tenacity of the post-Famine

Irish' and that his visit came at a most appropriate time, with the economic boom of the early 1960s. In his definitive study, *Ireland Since the Famine*, F.S.L. Lyons noted that the Kennedy visit had been triumphant and that in this period Ireland had a strong American orientation. Ronan Fanning has captured the sense of the occasion when he says the visit 'had a stunning impact.' 'The latter day Hero / Playboy of the Western World and the apotheosis of the returned Yank who had made good,' declared Fanning, 'Kennedy personified the wider ambitions of a new Ireland in which anything was possible.'

In his chronicle of Ireland in the 1960s, Fergal Tobin viewed the Kennedy visit essentially as closing the chapter on the famine era, a view shared by Ambassador Kiernan. As well, declares Tobin, Kennedy, like de Valera, had a definition of Irish nationalism that was 'unhistorical'. In fact, and this seems to have been forgotten by some, Kennedy had a three-part message in Ireland: pride in the past, celebration of present achievement and encouragement for the future. Yet the two major histories of modern Ireland produced in the 1980s — by Roy Foster and Joseph Lee — say nothing about Kennedy. American historians of Ireland give the subject scant treatment. In their recent survey, *The Irish Experience*, Thomas Hachey, Joseph Hernon and Lawrence McCaffrey simply compare the Kennedy visit with that of Ronald Reagan in 1984. Have these historians appropriately decided that this kind of thing should be relegated to popular history, folk memory, or was the Kennedy connection really unimportant after all?[17]

Kennedy did a great deal for both Irish people and those who were concerned with their Irish roots. He provided a magnificent example of achievement, both personal and political. No other leader since Franklin Roosevelt has inspired more people in more places. The wit, quest for knowledge, capacity, courage and sheer joy of life is remarkable. He put an international spotlight on the new, progressive Ireland that was emerging in the early 1960s.

An interesting question is what more he might have done for Ireland. He had established close personal relations with the Irish leaders — de Valera, Lemass, Aiken. His sense of Irish roots was fully awakened. The Irish Government had co-operated with his Administration in every matter of mutual interest. After he won re-election by a substantial margin, as was most likely, he would be in a strong position. He knew clearly what the prime concern of the Irish Government was. For the first time since independence it did not concern economic development. The early 1960s was a period of rapid economic growth. The prime concern of the Irish leaders was the underlying one of partition. De Valera, for one, had hoped that Kennedy would lend a hand in this vital matter during his second term. Surely he had some basis for this hope.[18]

What could a prudent and resourceful person like Kennedy have done? No one expected him to mount a platform to demand that the British get out of the Six Counties. What he could have done is press home, privately and diplomatically, to the British Government evidence of gross injustice towards the Catholic/nationalist population in Northern Ireland in the matters of employment, representation, civil rights and more. If he had already done that, in private chats with Harold Macmillan or whatever, there is no evidence of any British response. The UK Government was completely unprepared for the eruption in Northern Ireland in the late 1960s.

Would he have acted on this? Britain was the most important US ally in a dangerous world; it, too, had been completely co-operative with the US Government. Again, he knew what the Irish Government wanted; surely the Irish leaders eventually would have pressed for some action. Would he have served out eight years as President and have declined this request? Irish-American opinion would have weighed in on this matter. Could the Kennedys have stood the charge that they were false to their Irish heritage? John Fitzgerald Kennedy was not a person to ignore injustice when the evidence of it was piled in front of him. Perhaps the British Government might have seen the wisdom of dealing with a smouldering problem before it exploded, but British policy in the Six Counties in the last 25 years makes that seem unlikely.

Had he lived he surely would have returned to Ireland, probably several times, as he said he would. Observing Kennedy's interest in Irish property while he toured the country, Ambassador Kiernan got the impression that Kennedy was interested in acquiring a house or apartment. Perhaps after the presidency he might have written about the problem of partition and what went on in Northern Ireland. It was the kind of subject that appealed to a man who not only made history but also wrote it. It seems inconceivable that he would have let the America Ireland Foundation wither away. Fortunately, the cultural and educational connections between the two countries have increased over the years.[19]

Here was a leader who inspired the young to personal excellence and public service, who gave the world a sense of hope and renewal and who was a source of pride and enjoyment to those of his background and heritage.

Thirty years have passed. To borrow a bit from Pascal, it is not how little we had of Jack Kennedy, but how much. Sean, fear maith, go raibh maith agat, agus Dia duit / John, good man, thank you very much and God bless.

DOCUMENTS

*'Documents are the primary sources of history; they
are the means by which later generations draw close
to historical events and enter into the thoughts, fears
and hopes of the past.'*

John F. Kennedy
19 January 1963

Document 1 — *John F. Kennedy, 'Irish Bases Vital to Britain'.* New York Journal American, *2 February 1941.*

IRISH BASES VITAL TO BRITAIN

The following is written for the N.Y. Journal and American by John F. Kennedy, whose recent book "Why England Slept" has been hailed as a masterly analysis of Britain's errors during the period preceding the German air blitzkrieg. A son of Ambassador Joseph P. Kennedy, the author has visited England, Ireland and France since the start of the war.

Should Ireland give Naval and Air bases to England? Is Ireland by her refusal to do so sleeping the same sleep that brought England to the brink of disaster?

This is a question to which the American people are now giving keen attention. And it is very important that they do so because the position that America takes may have a great influence on the final settlement of this dispute.

It is obvious, of course, under present conditions that the British will hesitate to take any step that they feel would alienate a large portion of the American public.

Hesitates To Act

They realize that there are nearly thirty million Americans of Irish extraction and that there are many more who have followed Ireland's fight for freedom with tremendous sympathy.

With England's growing dependence on the American arsenal, she hesitates, unless forced by grim necessity, to take a step that might turn a large portion of American opinion against her.

In the same measure, Ireland under De Valera has been fighting in this country for support of her policy of neutrality. In Ireland's long struggle, the aid that poured from America has been decisive and the ties that bind the two countries together are as strong now as ever.

If the weight of American public opinion was to be turned against Ireland, De Valera's position might be compromised.

For America, itself, the question has also grave implications. President Roosevelt in his last two speeches has declared that Britain's survival is essential for America's security.

If this is true and if Ireland's present policy weakens Britain's chances, it naturally follows that we ourselves in America must be affected.

Thus, it is easy to see that this is no mere academic question that the American people are now facing. It is of vital importance. The decision may well affect the destinies of not only the people of Ireland and England, but of our own United States.

We should therefore try to judge the question as fairly as possible. Both sides must be given equal consideration. Racial ties and past bitterness should not influence our decision. In taking our position we must continually bear in mind the importance of what is involved.

Two-Sided Argument

On the one hand, it may mean a defenseless Ireland will be exposed to the horrors of the blitz war. On the other, it may mean calling upon England to carry a burden which may force her to her knees in defeat.

Let us look, therefore, at the arguments of the two sides with an open mind. First, the British case.

Foremost among the British arguments is the strong feeling that as Ireland's future independence is directly involved in this fight, she should be willing to aid Britain in her battle.

The British point out that should they go under, Ireland would quickly follow in the tragic path of Norway, Holland, Belgium, Denmark and the other small countries who thought their neutrality would preserve their independence.

They feel, therefore, that while England in the past may have been extremely slow about granting Ireland her freedom, yet Ireland does have it now. The only way for her to preserve it is to join wholeheartedly with England in her fight against Nazism.

They remind the Irish that the 'devil you know is better than the devil you don't', and that Ireland would stand a far better chance of living in peace and freedom in a world free from the menace of Hitler.

Strategic Importance

With this as a central theme the British put forward a number of arguments illustrating the decisive strategic importance of Ireland. They feel that Britain's strength would be tremendously increased if Ireland would give her naval and air bases.

The ports England is chiefly interested in are those of Queenstown or Cobh, Berehaven and Lough Swilly. These are the ports that were turned over to Ireland by the agreement of 1938.

While the southern route is not at present being used due to the German bases on the French West coast, the British feel that a naval and air base at Cobh would be of great help as a center of operations against the German-held ports.

Berehaven and Lough Swilly (as can be seen on the map) would be of much greater importance. Berehaven, especially, would give the British a base 200 miles west of any that they have at present, and this; they feel, would make a tremendous difference in the success of the convoy system.

British planes based in these ports could fly much further out to sea in search for submarines, and could counteract the planes that serve as spotters for the German undersea raiders.

Blocking the Gateway

With more and more supplies promised from America, the British feel that the further protection that British shipping might obtain could well prove decisive. Ireland in her present position is blocking the gateway from the New World to the Old.

Another powerful argument of the British is that unless they are given an opportunity to establish bases in the Free State, it would not be an impos-sible task for the Germans, striking swiftly, to establish themselves before England could move to counteract it.

Though such a move presents obvious difficulties, yet the Norway experience ever before them, the British hate to see a situation developing which might bring with it a repetition of that disaster.

The Irish Viewpoint

These briefly are the chief British arguments. In opposition to these the Irish have presented an equally impressive case. The fundamental Irish argument is that to give the British these bases would mean the involvement of Ireland in a war for which they are completely unprepared.

The Irish Government feels that its first and fundamental duty is to its own people. Except for extremists, of course, the Irish are completely sympathetic with the British cause.

They do realize that the future of Ireland as an independent state may be threatened if the Nazis win; but on the other hand they do not feel that Ireland's independence would be guaranteed if the British reoccupied the present Free State.

It must be remembered that the British quarrel with Ireland has been going on for over six hundred years, while the German-British fight is a comparatively modern one.

Remember the Past

In addition, Ireland has bitter memories of the last war. England made large promises to Ireland at that time in return for her support and Ireland paid a tragic price — she sent a greater number of soldiers in proportion to her population than any other unit of the British Empire. And except for France, this army suffered a greater percentage of killed and wounded than any other country in the war.

For this great sacrifice the Irish received nothing. Instead the Lloyd George Government, in which Winston Churchill was Minister for War, dispatched the Black and Tans who scourged Ireland for three years.

Ireland has not forgotten this, and remembers further that in 1938 Mr. Churchill also led the group who opposed the return of the ports to Ireland. They do not feel they can depend on him to restore them once the war is over.

They feel, also, that when Parliament voted its approval in 1938 of their release it did so with the full knowledge that Ireland would remain neutral if a European war began.

Persistent Silence

In regard to the ports themselves, the Irish argue that they are by no means of decisive importance. Cobh would do England little actual good as the British have mined the Southern Channel and no shipping is going that route.

Lough Swilly is not essential either as the British have a port just twenty miles to the eastward in Northern Ireland. Berehaven might prove of more value, but the Irish do not feel that the possession of it would be the difference, by any means, between British success and failure.

Another important argument is the persistent silence of the British regarding any post-war solution of the Partition problem.

Of course it must be pointed out that De Valera reportedly has stated that Neutrality for Ireland is now more important than Union. That he should thus reject an opportunity to fulfill his life-long ambition is, his supporters say, conclusive evidence of his deep sincerity.

Yet even if this is so, that the British have seemingly made no attempts to settle this problem, causes the Irish to wonder if the British have given up all hope of again exerting control over the Free State.

Unwilling to Join in

With these feelings as a background, the Irish feel unwilling to join the struggle. At best they feel the price Ireland would pay would be terrific, and if England were defeated she would be placed in a far worse position.

Ireland therefore feels that the United States has no right to ask her to take such a grave step. She points out that the United States itself has refused to fight, and she feels it would be most unfair for America to urge her to take a course of action that would mean war.

Though she hopes to remain neutral she will continue to aid England in every possible way, but she will resist with all her power any attempt by either of the belligerents to force her to change her neutral policy.

Here then are the highlights of the arguments on both sides, about which volumes could be written. Here then is the dilemma — and the American people must realize that the attitude that they take may prove of great importance:

Should Ireland give up the ports and take the risk of undergoing the horrors of modern war?

It is hard to foretell the solution.

Will the Irish change their policy of neutrality in favor of Britain if they feel it might prove of decisive importance? Will the British if hard pressed risk Irish opposition and forcibly take the ports and bases over. The next few months should give the answer.

Document 2 — *John F. Kennedy, 'De Valera Aims to Unite Ireland'*. New York Journal American, *29 July 1945*

DE VALERA AIMS TO UNITE IRELAND

(John F. Kennedy, former Navy lieutenant in command of a P-T boat, decorated for bravery in action, is in Europe writing on various matters of worldwide interest. He is the son of former Ambassador Joseph P. Kennedy, and before the war was author of the best seller "Why England Slept".)

London, July 26. When the tall angular figure of Mr. De Valera rose in the Irish Dail to answer Mr. James Dillon's question about Ireland's constitutional status with the words 'We are a Republic', world attention turned once again to Ireland.

For the question immediately arose, 'How could Ireland be a republic and at the same time a member of the British Commonwealth of nations, the connecting link of which was a common allegiance to the British Crown?'

In the debate that followed a week later, De Valera's elaboration of his remarks left the situation to many observers as misty as this island on an early Winter's morning.

'Ireland', said De Valera, 'was an independent republic associated as a matter of external policy with the states of the British Commonwealth.'

She was a republic because the head of the Irish state was a president chosen by the free vote of the people.

The King of England was not the King of Ireland. He was merely the method of marking the association between Ireland and other members of the British Commonwealth.

As to whether Ireland itself was a member of the British Commonwealth, De Valera quoted a statement issued by the British Government in 1937 to the effect that Ireland was — and left it at that.

Why was it there should be this enigmatic explanation in these cautious words carefully weighed after weeks of study?

And why did Mr. Dillon press his questions with such persistence? To find the answer to these questions is to know the fundamental motivating force behind Irish politics. There is nothing new about this force.

Every Irishman, wherever in the world he may be, knows what it is. It is the age-old quarrel with England, once fought in Dail and council chambers.

Sheridan once said, 'A quarrel is a very pretty quarrel as it stands. We should only spoil it by trying to explain it.'

Without attempting to go back into the history of it, the quarrel is worth examining at the present time because it not only explains the verbal exchange between De Valera and Dillon, but it explains the reasons for De Valera's past actions, and with an understanding of it, his future course can be chartered.

Ireland at the present time is divided into two distinct political units — the 26 counties of the south, which comprise present day Eire, and the six counties in the north, known as Ulster, which are attached directly to the British Crown.

De Valera is determined to end this partition, as it is called, and to that cause he has dedicated his life.

In this cause, all Irishmen of the south are united.

On this there is no dispute between Dillon and De Valera.

The dispute concerns the method to be followed.

Dillon and Gen. Mulcahy, leader of the Fine Gael Party, Ireland's second largest political party, argue it is time to bury old hatchets.

England and Ireland are bound together by the closest economic ties.

Militarily, England will never consent to see a completely neutral and weakly armed power on her vulnerable western flank.

Only if England has a guarantee that this and other bases are put at her disposal, in case of war, will she consent to give up her great base of Ulster, which served her so well in this war.

By cooperating and the building of mutual trust, the partition can be broken and all Ireland united.

So argue Dillon and a substantial section of the Irish populace.

But ranged against this group is the powerful Fianna Fail Party, led by the brilliant, austere figure of De Valera, born in New York, the son of a Spanish father and an Irish mother.

De Valera is fighting politically the same relentless battle they fought in the field during the uprising of 1916, in the war of independence and later in the civil war.

He feels everything Ireland has gained has been given grudgingly and at the end of a long and bitter struggle.

Always it has been too little and too late.

He is surrounded by men of the same background in his government. They include Sean Lemass, deputy prime minister, Sean MacEntee, chief of the local government, Gerald Boland, minister of justice, and Dr. Ryan, minister of agriculture. Many were in the abortive uprising of 1916. All fought in the war of independence against the Black and Tans and later in the civil war of 1922.

All have been in both Engl[ish] and Irish prisons, and many have wounds which still ache when the cold rains come in from the west. They have not forgotten nor have they forgiven.

The only settlement they will accept is a free and independent Ireland, free to go where it will be the master of its own destiny.

Only on these terms will they accept the ending of the partition. Thus, there are two splits.

One is a strong stand and supported by the great majority of the people. The other is willing to compromise in view of present world circumstances and willing to join the commonwealth and work with it. Thus we begin to see behind the debate of De Valera and Dillon these two viewpoints.

Dillon is attempting to pin De Valera to being completely in or completely out of the British Commonwealth and thus make political capital, no matter what decision he makes.

On the other hand, De Valera, realizing how subtle his position is and not wishing to alienate those who advocate a complete break with Britain, yet conscious of the fact that only with Britain's support can the partition be ended, is skating along thin ice successfully with his enigmatic reply.

In the north, Sir Basil Brooke, head of the government in Ulster, listened to be debate and roared down to the gentlemen in Dublin that 'not an inch' will be give(n) up of the six counties.

And in the south, De Valera hurled back the challenge that from his present position he will retreat 'not an inch'.

At this weekend, the problem of partition seems very far from being solved.

Document 3 — *Extract from JFK Speech. 'England,
Ireland and Germany: Victor, Neutral, Vanquished'*

11 NOVEMBER 1945, CROSSCUP-PISHON AMERICAN LEGION POST
PRE-PRESIDENTIAL PAPERS, BOX 94, KENNEDY LIBRARY

*O**ur foreign policy today may well determine the kind of
life we will live here for generations. For peace and
prosperity of this country are truly indivisible from the
peace and prosperity of the world in this atomic age.*

*But before we whole-heartedly subscribe to any foreign policy,
it may be well for us to examine the kinds of governments that
are taking over in the countries of post-war Europe and try to
estimate where they are headed. I would like to offer for your
consideration today my personal observations on three of these
countries — England, Ireland and Germany — victor, neutral
and vanquished. . . .*

*I propose today to discuss one of these countries — Ireland —
because I think its relationship with England is typical of the
many problems which England will be facing in the future with
increasing regularity.*

*The world's attention was turned to Ireland last July by a
debate in the Irish Dail between Prime Minister De Valera and
Mr. James Dillon. For when Mr. De Valera answered Mr. Dillon's
question concerning Eire's constitutional status with the words,
'We are a Republic', it immediately raised the question of whether
or not Eire was a member of the British Commonwealth of
nations, the connecting link of which is a common allegiance to
the British crown.*

*Mr. De Valera waited a week before he answered this question.
The world waited with him. When the answer finally came, it left
many observers somewhat bewildered, but it neatly extracted
Mr. De Valera from a very precarious political position. He did
not say whether or not he believed that Eire was a member of the
British Commonwealth of nations. He merely quoted a British
statement of 1931 to the effect that she was — and left it at that.
Why these careful words, this guarded reply after a week of study?*

*Behind the debate of Mr. Dillon and Mr. De Valera loomed the
fundamental problem behind all Irish politics — the problem of
ending the partition, which divides the twenty-six counties of the*

south, which form Eire, and the six counties of the north known as Ulster which are attached directly to Great Britain. That this partition must be ended both Mr. De Valera and Mr. Dillon agree. On this all Irishmen agree. The dispute lies in the method to be followed.

A great many people in Eire feel that the only way to end partition is to come to an agreement with the British, to take a full part in the British Commonwealth of nations, and to make a treaty of mutual defense. They argue that the British will not tolerate a sullen neutral on their vulnerable western flank. Rather than have this, the British will support the government in Ulster until the end of time. This is the view of the Fine Gael or United Ireland Party formerly led by Cosgrave and now by that able warrior who proved his toughness in the wars against the Black and Tans, General Mulcahy.

The day that I called on General Mulcahy he was sitting in a small office surrounded by books, but he looked like the soldier he was. He was a man of strong opinions. When an Irish politician gives you his views on his country's position, you know that they are not lightly held and that he has probably shed some blood in their defense. The most impressive object in General Mulcahy's room is a large picture of Michael Collins. We spent only a few minutes talking about the General and several hours talking about Collins.

This young man who was killed in his early thirties looms as large today in Ireland as when he died. As General Mulcahy said, 'If Michael Collins had lived, the history of Ireland would be different.' Collins, who died in the Civil War of 1922, was only one of the many brilliant young Irishmen who died in what Kevin O'Higgins called 'the spilling of the wine'.

But against the party of General Mulcahy is ranged the powerful Fianna Fail 'Soldiers of Ireland' which now holds a majority in the Irish Dail. This is the party of De Valera who fought Cosgrave and Collins in 1922 until finally defeated and who now continues the battle in the Dail. These are the men who claim that everything that Ireland has ever gotten from England has been only at the end of a long and bitter struggle. Always it has been too little and too late. This is the party of De Valera, and in his government he is surrounded by men of the same tough fiber. All have been in British and Irish prisons and *many of them have wounds which still ache when the cold rains come in from the west.*

One of these is Frank Gallagher, De Valera's secretary. Instead of the hundreds and hundreds of young men in our OWI and in the British Ministry of Information, in Eire there is just one man, Gallagher, and he is a gold mine of information. He has been with De Valera for many years and fought in the war against the British and in the Civil War. One evening when I had been talking with him for hours, I said, 'Frank, I think I'm taking up too much of your time.'

He replied, 'My boy, I have the best job in the world. I am the only man in Ireland who gets paid for just talking.'

Mr. Dillon, an independent who supports the opposition to Mr. De Valera, was attempting to demonstrate in his debate with De Valera that Eire's constitutional position was, as he put it, like that of a cat which has its tail caught in the door — neither in nor out — and in a state of considerable intellectual perplexity.'

He feels that Eire today is bound to England with the closest of economic bonds. England today buys more than 90 per cent of Eire's exports. England also owes Eire over 400,000,000 pounds sterling, which makes Eire one of the wealthiest nations proportionally in the world. This balance was built up during the war when Eire supplied Britain with food on credit.

Economically and strategically Eire is bound to England, argues Mr. Dillon. It is only nursing ancient quarrels long since dead for Mr. De Valera to consistently hold to his position that he will make no commitments of any nature until Ireland is united under the flag of Eire.

But at the present time De Valera holds the whip hand.

The Irish are as vigorous in their support of De Valera's policy of neutrality as they are proud of the thousands and thousands of young men who left their country to join the British army. And to those critics who wonder whether the Irish are getting soft, they point to the seven Victoria Crosses, England's highest decoration, won by soldiers from the Southern counties. They take singular pleasure in the fact that in spite of their close ties to England, there were none won by the soldiers from Ulster.

De Valera has a unique hold on the hearts of the Irish people. The fact that it was De Valera who made the deal that returned the now famous ports of Berehaven, Queenstown and Lough

Swilly to Eire gives them confidence that it will be De Valera who will finally settle the problem of Partition. He has always won support for his policies by appealing to the strong patriotic instinct of all Irishmen. Thus he won support for his policy of neutrality during the war by identifying neutrality with freedom from England, which will always win support.

There is no compromise in De Valera's firm, ascetic face. He has a passionate intensity and single-mindedness in the course he is taking that brooks no opposition. He is extremely conscious that his visit to the German Legation on Hitler's death caused unfavourable comment in America. He discussed it with me at some length. He was determined to carry out Eire's policy of strict neutrality to the end, and carry it out he did. To all critics he answers, 'I kept Ireland out of the war.'

Eire at the present time has a unique political set-up. There is no 'left' party in the accepted sense. The 'left' in Eire are not those who favor more and more governmental control, as in France for example, but are those who favor a complete break with England; the right — those who believe in working with England in the Commonwealth. De Valera walks a tightrope between the two extremes. While in his heart he is far to the left, yet he realizes that economically and strategically Eire is bound by the strongest ties to England and that only with England's support can Partition be ended. His vague answer to Mr. Dillon's question about Ireland's position in the British Commonwealth, in the debate referred to before, clearly demonstrates his delicate position.

As to the possibility of his ending Partition, no one can say. Sir Alan Brooke, head of the government in Ulster, recently roared down to the gentlemen in Dublin that 'not an inch' will he give up of the six counties of the North. And it is somewhat dubious if England, after its narrow escape during this conflict, will ever consent to giving up her naval base at Belfast until she at least has assurances of support in case of another war. Some people feel that General Mulcahy and Mr. Dillon, with their willingness to play a full part in the British Commonwealth, may yet be the ones to end Partition. . . .

Document 4 — *JFK account of 1947 visit to Wexford*

PRESIDENT'S OFFICE FILES, PERSONAL SECRETARY'S FILES, BOX 129, FOLDER: 'BOOKS — JFK, A POLITICAL PROFILE'. KENNEDY LIBRARY, BOSTON.

August 25, 1959

Professor Jim Burns
Williams College
Williamstown, Massachusetts

Dear Jim:
    In regard to some information on my visit to New Ross, my sister and I had taken Lismore Castle in County Waterford, Ireland, in the month of August. The castle belonged to the Devonshire family. The people staying with us at the castle were Sean Leslie — an Irish writer and character, Hugh Fraser, M.P., Anthony Eden, Mrs. Randolph Churchill, etc.
    I had received a letter from an old aunt giving me directions as to where in New Ross the Kennedys had come from. I drove over for one day with an English lady and followed the directions, which turned out to be quite exact. I drove up a small lane and asked an Irishman standing on the side of the road where the Kennedys lived. He told me to drive up a hundred yards and turn to the right. It was a middle-sized Irish farmhouse, thatch roof, near a stream. We drove in and sure enough, a Kennedy family was living in the house which had been described to us in my aunt's letter. There was a husband and wife and seven or eight children — all very bright and very energetic. We were greeted with friendliness, especially as they had never seen a station wagon before, but they had no idea which of the Kennedys I was. The farmer did say that a Patrick Kennedy from Boston, who of course was my grandfather, had come to visit the home some thirty-five years before when the farmer was a boy. They kept asking me if I were related to a Jim Kennedy or an Edward Kennedy who had gone to New York some years ago. It sounded from their conversation as if all the Kennedys had emigrated. I figured that they were my third cousins.

I spent about an hour there surrounded by chickens, pigs, etc., and left in a flow of nostalgia and sentiment. This was not punctured by the English lady turning to me as we drove off and saying, 'Just like Tobacco Road.' She had not understood at all the magic of the afternoon. We returned to Lismore Castle.

Best regards,
John F. Kennedy

Document 5 — *Resolution on Irish unification,*
sponsored by Kennedy and others, US Senate, 1957

JFK PRE-PRESIDENTIAL PAPERS, SENATE FILE, LEGISLATION, 1956–57,
BOX 670, KENNEDY LIBRARY.

That it is the sense of the Senate of the United States that the
maintenance of international peace and security requires
settlement of the question of the unification of Ireland and
that the people of all Ireland, including the people of Eire and
the people of Northern Ireland, should have a free opportunity
to express their will for union and that this be attained by an
election of the people of all Ireland under the auspices of a
United Nations Commission for Ireland, to be designated by
the General Assembly pursuant to articles 11 and 35 of the
Charter, which shall establish the terms and conditions of
such election with the objective of the entry of Ireland as a
member of the United Nations.

Document 6 — *JFK statement in support of resolution in House of Representatives*

CONGRESSIONAL RECORD, VOL. 97, PART. 9, 27 SEPTEMBER 1951.

I rise in support of this resolution which, if it passes, would be an important step forward toward the unification of Ireland. It would initiate action that would do much to end an ancient injustice and is in accordance with the traditional American support of self-determination.

Ireland's fight for national unity and independence is over 700 years old. It is a fight that cannot be considered won until the 6 counties of the north are reunited with the 26 counties that now comprise Eire.

A free, united integrated Ireland would provide an important bastion for the defense of the west, and would contribute to the strategic security of the United States.

Document 7 — *JFK Visit to Dublin, 1955.*
Irish Independent, *1 October 1955*

U.S. SENATOR VISITS DUBLIN

Sen. J.F. Kennedy, the youngest member of the U.S. Senate who is in Dublin for a three days visit, is the second eldest son of Mr. J.P. Kennedy, Ambassador in London between 1937 and 1941.

Yesterday the Senator and his wife were entertained to luncheon by Mr. Cosgrave, Minister for External Affairs.

In the afternoon Senator Kennedy visited All Hallowes, where he addressed the students on the position of the Catholic Church in Poland, which he visited recently. The Church, he said, was the great obstacle to the spread of Russian domination and the churches were never more crowded than at present.

In his opinion, the concessions made by the Communists at Geneva were merely superficial: the basic domination remained the same.

Aged 38, Senator Kennedy has been a member of the Senate since 1952, and prior to that was a Congressman for six years. His last visit to Ireland was six years ago.

He hopes to attend a race meeting today.

Document 8 — *JFK St. Patrick's Day Speech,
Irish Fellowship Club of Chicago, March 17, 1956.
With JFK additions { } and deletions [ ].*

PRE-PRESIDENTIAL FILES, SPEECH FILES, BOX 895, KENNEDY
LIBRARY.

I am glad to be here tonight because I feel strongly the ties of a common kinship. All of us of Irish descent are bound together by the ties that come from a common experience, experience which may exist only in memories and in legend, but which is real enough to those who possess it. And thus whether we live in Cork or Boston, Chicago or Sydney, we are all members of a great family which is linked together by that strongest of chains — a common past. It is strange to think that the wellspring from which this fraternal empire has sprung is a small island in the far Atlantic with a population one-third the size of that of this prairie state. But this is the source, and it is to this green and misty island that we turn tonight and to its patron saint, Saint Patrick.

{Perhaps one of the strongest threads that runs through our common past is the willingness to make any sacrifice for liberty.}

It is also fitting that we remember tonight three requests granted St. Patrick by the Angel of the Lord, in order to bring happiness and hope to the Irish: first, that the weather should always be fair on his special day to allow the faithful to attend the services of the church; second, that every Thursday and every Saturday twelve souls of the Irish people should be freed from the pains of Hell; and third, that no outlander should ever rule over Ireland.

I have not heard a weather report from the Emerald Isle tonight, but I am certain that no rain fell — officially. Who pays any heed to a little Irish mist? And I have no doubt that twelve Irishmen have been freed from the nether regions this very Saturday. In fact, the toastmaster tells me he thinks he saw several of them here tonight. But certainly we need no report to tell us that tonight no outlander rules over Eire; and the Irish people are celebrating this day in peace and in liberty.

But is it not a bitter and tragic irony that the Irish should now enjoy their freedom at a time when [hundreds of millions] are held in an iron captivity in areas stretching in a great half circle from the plains beyond the captive city of Warsaw in the West to the Red River Delta beyond the trampled city of Hanoi in the East. For as the Irish have finally emerged from the shadow of subjugation, the eclipse of a new Age of Tyranny has darkened the skies of many ancient states which had enjoyed a long history of personal liberty and national independence. [Today, while free Irishmen everywhere marched to the tune of 'O'Donnell Abu' and 'The Irish Captain', only hobnailed boots clattering on darkened streets rang out in these enslaved nations.]

I know of few men in our land, and none in this room, who would ignore these tyrannies as far-off troubles of no concern at home. For we realize, as John Boyle O'Reilly once wrote, that:

> *The world is large, when its weary leagues*
> *two loving hearts divide;*
> *But the world is small, when your enemy*
> *is loose on the other side.*

I do not maintain that the Irish were the only race to display extraordinary devotion to liberty, or the only people to struggle unceasingly for their national independence. History proves otherwise. But the special contribution of the Irish, I believe — the emerald thread that runs throughout the tapestry of their past — has been the constancy, the endurance, the faith that they displayed through endless centuries of foreign oppression — centuries in which even the most rudimentary religious and civil rights were denied to them.

For all the classic weapons of oppression were employed to break the will of the Irish. Religious persecution was encouraged — mass starvation was ignored. On February 19, 1847, it was announced in the House of Commons that 15,000 persons were dying of starvation in Ireland every day; and Queen Victoria was so moved by this pitiful news that she contributed five pounds to the society for Irish relief. [We should not be too quick to condemn the good Queen — for in those days the English pound was no doubt worth more than it is today.]

Even assassination was employed to end resistance. Listen, if you will, to the wild melancholy of the Irish after the after the murder by Cromwell's agents of their beloved Chieftain, Owen Roe O'Neill:

> *Sagest in the council was he; kindest in the hall;*
> *Sure we never won a battle — 'twas Owen won them all.*
> *Soft as woman's was your voice, O'Neill, bright was your eye.*
> *Oh! why did you leave us, Owen? Why did you die?*
> *Your troubles are all over, you're at rest with God on high;*
> *But we're slaves, and we're orphans, Owen! — why did you die?*
> *We're sheep without a shepherd, when the snow shuts out the sky —*
> *Oh! Why did you leave us, Owen! Why did you die?*

It is not my purpose to recall needlessly the unhappy memories of an age gone by. But I think that the history of the Irish — and indeed of all people, East and West — demonstrates that along with the need to worship God there has been implanted in every man's soul the desire to be free.

The greatest enemy today of man's desire to be free is, of course, the Soviet Union, which holds its captives in a subjugation hard and unending, maintained by a tyranny more sinister and persuasive than any in the history of the world. The United States and her allies have for more than a decade been attempting to halt this Communist advance. But one of the weaknesses in our common front has been the restraint on freedom sponsored by our allies and accepted by ourselves.

For the sake of our own security, we have found our destiny to be closely linked with that of the British and the French, the Dutch and the Belgians, (and the Portuguese) — nations which still hold under the subjugation large areas of the world upon which they feel their ultimate security depends.

And thus we have been caught up in a dilemma which up to now has been insoluble. We want our allies to be strong, and yet quite obviously a part of their strength comes from their overseas possessions. And thus our dilemma has become a paradox. We fight to keep the world free from Communist imperialism — but in doing so we hamper our efforts, and bring suspicion upon our motives, by being closely linked with Western imperialism. We have permitted the reputation of the United States as a friend of oppressed people to be hitched to the chariot of the conqueror, because we believed we could have it both ways.

It is easy for us to believe that the imperialism of the West is infinitely preferable to the totalitarianism of the Soviets — but the sullen hostility of Islam and Asia should make us wonder. We thought it would be obvious to the North African that control by France is better for the North Africans than control by the Communists. I happen to believe it is — but I do not live in North Africa. When Stalin was alive and personified aggression — in a hurry and on the make — it was possible for natives to see the true meaning of Communist control. But now, in a period when the Communist challenge is more subtle, when they employ the people's passions for freedom by skillfully manipulating native leaders, our position has become [more difficult].

I do not wish to over simplify an endlessly complex problem, nor deny the success we have had in helping free nations remain free. But our attempts to look both ways on the subject of colonialism has caused our standing in the free world to be seriously questioned. The time has come for a more forceful stand.

I urge, therefore, that this nation, acting within appropriate limits of judgement and discretion, inform our allies and the world at large that — after a reasonable period of transition and self-determination — this nation will speak out boldly for freedom for all people — whether they are denied that freedom by an iron curtain of tyranny, or by the paper curtain of colonial ties and constitutional manipulations. We shall no longer abstain in the U.N. from voting on colonial issues — we shall no longer trade our vote on such issues for other supposed gains — we shall no longer seek to prevent the subjugated peoples of the world from being heard and we shall recognize that the day of the colonial is through, and that words of lasting wisdom were printed nearly 160 years ago by the imprisoned editor of the Dublin Press, *Arthur O'Connor:*

'If there be any man so base or so stupid', wrote Arthur O'Connor in his Address to the Irish Nation, 'as to imagine that they can usurp or withhold your civil and political rights; that they can convert truth into sedition or patriotism into treason, let them look around them. They will find that amongst the old and inveterate despotisms in Europe, some have been destroyed and the rest are on the brink of destruction.'

Such a warning is no less true today, as one by one the traditional colonies of Western powers break free. Only a bold and sympathetic stand by the United States during this period of transition will prevent them from falling under the control of a tyranny infinitely more infamous than that from which they are now emerging.

You may feel that this has little to do with Ireland and the Irish, but we must not forget that freedom is the commodity the Irish have valued most highly and the commodity that Ireland has exported most widely. The 'wild geese' — the Irish officers and soldiers who fled Ireland after the Battle of the Boyne — fought for freedom in all parts of the world. Exiled, persecuted and loyal, they and their descendants fought in their part of the world for their outlawed religion, their denationalised country and their hopes for freedom. Fighting for the French, they broke the ranks of the English at Fontenoy. Fighting for the Spanish, they turned the tide of battle against the Germans at Melaszo. And fighting for the Union Army, they bore the brunt of the slaughter at Fredericksburg.

> *[War-battered dogs are we*
> *Gnawing a naked bone;*
> *Fighting in every land and clime*
> *For every cause but our own.]*

Thus Irishmen today can sympathize with the aspirations of all people everywhere to be free — and their long and ultimately successful fight for independence offers encouragement and hope to all who struggle to be free. Let the United States and all free people today speak to captive peoples everywhere with the words of Sir Roger Casement as he addressed the British jury which had sentenced him to hang for high treason in 1914: 'When all your fights', said Sir Roger, 'become only an accumulated wrong, when men must beg with bated breath for leave to subsist in their own land, to think their own thoughts, to sing their own songs — then surely it is a braver, a saner and a truer thing to be a rebel in act and in deed. Gentlemen of the Jury: Ireland has outlived the failure of her hopes — and yet she still hopes. And this fact — of preserving through centuries of misery the remembrance of lost liberty — this surely is the noblest cause men ever strove for, ever lived for, ever died for. If this be the case for

*which I stand indicted here today, then I stand in a goodly
company and in a right noble succession.'*

*[There is our message, Mr. President. There is our faith and
our task. Let us not foil its fulfillment. Let us hold out our hands
to those who struggle for freedom today as Ireland struggled for
a thousand years. Let us not leave them to be sheep without a
shepherd when the snow shuts out the sky'. Let us show them
we have not forgotten the constancy and the faith and the hope
of the Irish.]*

Document 9 — *John F. Kennedy, A Nation of Immigrants — extract (New York, 1964, with an introduction by Robert F. Kennedy)*

BASED ON A SPEECH BY KENNEDY TO NEW YORK CHAPTER OF B'NAI B'RITH IN 1958, IT WAS PUBLISHED AS A FORTY-PAGE BOOKLET THAT YEAR. AN ENLARGED EDITION APPEARED IN 1964.

Waves of Immigration — the Post-Revolutionary Forces

A merican independence, the spreading westward of the new nation, the beginnings of economic diversification and industrialization, all these factors gave immigration in the nineteenth century a new context and a new role. The gates were now flung open, and men and women in search of a new life came to these shores in ever-increasing numbers — 150,000 in the 1820s, 1.7 million in the 1840s, 2.8 million in the 1870s, 5.2 million in the 1880s, 8.8 million in the first decade of the twentieth century. And, as the numbers increased, the sources changed. As the English had predominated in the seventeenth and eighteenth centuries, so the Irish and Germans predominated in the first half of the nineteenth and the Italians and Eastern Europeans in the last part of the nineteenth and the early part of the twentieth centuries. Each new wave of immigration helped meet the needs of American development and made its distinctive contribution to the American character.

The Irish

The Irish were in the vanguard of the great waves of immigration to arrive during the nineteenth century. By 1850, after the potato famine, they had replaced England as the chief source of new settlers, making up 44 percent of the foreign-born in the United States. In the century between 1820 and 1920, some four and a quarter million people left Ireland to come to the United States.

They were mostly country folk, small farmers, cottagers and farm laborers. Yet they congregated mainly in cities along the

Eastern seaboard, for they did not have the money to travel after reaching shore. Few could read or write; some spoke only Gaelic.

The Irish were the first to endure the scorn and discrimination later to be inflicted, to some degree at least, on each successive wave of immigrants by already settled 'Americans'. In speech and dress they seemed foreign; they were poor and unskilled; and they were arriving in overwhelming numbers. The Irish are perhaps the only people in our history with the distinction of having a political party, the Know-Nothings, formed against them. Their religion was later also the target of the American Protective Association and, in this century, the Klu Klux Klan.

The Irish found many doors closed to them, both socially and economically. Advertisements for jobs specified: 'No Irish need apply'. But there was manual labor to be done, and the Irish were ready to do it. They went to work as longshoreman, as ditch-diggers or as construction workers. When their earnings were not enough to support their families, their wives and daughters obtained employment as servants.

Contractors usually met them at the dock. The Erie Canal, linking New York with the Great Lakes in 1825, and other canals in Massachusetts, New Jersey, Pennsylvania and Maryland were largely built by Irish labor. But the canals soon became obsolete, and the frenzied building of railroads followed. In the three decades from 1830 to 1860, a network of thirty thousand miles of rails were laid across the middle of the country. Again Irish labor furnished the muscle. When railroad construction was pushed westward in the latter part of the century, the Irish again figured prominently, by now as foremen and section bosses. They also provided, at the same time, a supply of cheap labor for the mills of Rhode Island and Massachusetts and the coal mines of Pennsylvania.

But as the years passed and new generations were born, things began to change. Gradually, rung by rung, the Irish climbed up the economic and social ladder. Some settled on farms, especially along the canals they had dug. But it was in the cities that they found their principal outlet, in areas in which they could demonstrate their abilities of self-expression, of administration and organization. They gravitated first into law and from that into politics and government. Having experienced for themselves the handicaps of illiteracy, they were determined that their children would have the advantages of education. To that end, they not only started parochial schools, but founded such institutions of higher learning as Notre Dame, Fordham, Holy Cross, Villanova, St. Louis University, Catholic University and Georgetown. They became teachers, writers, journalists, labor organizers, orators and priests. As an expanding society offered more opportunities, they swelled not only the civil service rosters, but the ranks of clerical and administrative workers in industry.

The Irish eased the way for other immigrant groups and speeded their assimilation in several ways. They firmly established the Catholic Church, originally French on this continent, as an English-speaking institution. The schools they founded offer educational opportunities to children of later immigrants of other tongues. The Irish had their own press, their own fraternal orders and their own charitable organizations.

Irish labor leaders fought for the rights of other groups as well as their own. Workers of Irish descent helped organize the Knights of Labor, the first big national union, which was a forerunner of the American Federation of Labor.

Document 10 — *Brendan Behan to JFK*

Presidential Office Files, box 119a, Kennedy Library

Algonquin Hotel
New York City
15.7.61

A Divine Vassal
   I would not be so presumptous (Sic) as to comment on
matters appertaining to the Relationship Between presidents
and prelates but I think the following anecdote about the 15th
century head of your maternal clan might interest from a
genealogical point of view: MacZeralk, larla Fitzgerald, Earl of
Kildare, poet, soldier known as the MacZeralk Mor — or the
Great Fitzgerald — was summoned to Rome to explain his
conduct in Burning the Cathedral. The Pope asked why he had
committed this enormous sacrilege. His Lordship replied: 'I
declare to Jesus, Your holiness, I would never have done it But
I thought the archbishop was inside.'
   I saw you speak in 7th Avenue and a man said to me,
'Even Mencken would have voted for him.'
                                    Brendan Behan

Document 11 — *Ambassador Thomas J. Kiernan on Kennedy and partition of Ireland*

T. J. KIERNAN ORAL HISTORY TRANSCRIPT, KENNEDY LIBRARY

KIERNAN: I said of course that I'd never troubled him to take any line or make any intervention with Mr. [Harold] Macmillan in the matter of the partition problem, which is our major problem. And he said he understood that. It would embarrass him because naturally with the special relationship between the British and American governments, that would have put the American government — perhaps it could have got him into a difficulty. At any rate, it hadn't been raised. I told him then that we didn't expect him to make any reference to the matter when he came to Ireland in his speech. His major speech was to the Parliament here to the Dail, and in the ordinary way on account of the relevance and the importance of this partition business, it would have been mentioned, I suppose, by a visiting statesman. And to avoid embarrassment on his own foreign relations I told him that we didn't expect anything. Presumably he would talk privately to the ministers here, but that was another matter.

O'CONNOR: Have you ever talked to him at all or mentioned to him at all the problem of partition? Had he ever said anything about it before?

KIERNAN: Yes. He asked me what could be done. And I said, 'Well, what do you think is the issue?' And he said, 'Well of course its an Irish issue.' I said, 'Well, that is of course the British line very good. But partition was enforced against the wishes of both parts of Ireland by the British. No country cuts itself in two.' And that took him aback. He said, 'That's quite true, of course, it is a British issue.' I said, 'The fact that the British are constantly in financial difficulties and yet subsidize the position in Northern Ireland at the rate of a hundred to a hundred and fifty million dollars a year indicates that they have an interest in perpetuating it.' And he did ask me to explain what I thought about the position, and I did go into it a bit with him. How difficult it is to get rid of old notions — the old notion that Britain had, that she needed her for self-

defense, to have a foothold in Ireland, that that disappeared
with the atomic bomb, with modern weapons of defense and
offense. And finally I said that what we would like and all that
we would ask is that some British spokesman should say that
it is not contrary to British interests if Ireland became united.
That after all is putting it in a very minimum way. And he
said, 'Well why, why should you — what value is that? I said,
'The value is that partition remains because the junta in the
six counties feel they have — they know they have — the
moral support of Britain. If a statement were made by the
British government that it would not be contrary to imperial
or to British interests if the country becomes united under a
single government they'd begin to get shaky in the moral
support, quite apart from the financial support. And he said,
'Well, you know it's very hard. I can see the British difficulty.
It's very hard to say that on account of the past history.' We
left it rather like that. You see, President Kennedy was, and
this is putting it much too extreme but its no harm to put it
like that, apart from his Americanism which was a hundred
percent, was more British than Irish.

O'CONNOR: That's a very interesting statement. Would you
explain that a little?

KIERNAN: I mean he had — I suppose it's the New England attitude in him, I suppose it's the Harvard attitude. And then those
with Irish names in America are still wanting to be accepted
as part of the establishment, or at any rate not be regarded as
outsiders. And then of course the British, the white Anglo-
Saxon, et ceteras are still regarded as almost incapable of
doing wrong. I'm afraid that is the position, that there is a
certain bias there which nothing can deplete. Kennedy's first
reaction would be, if there were any even minor dispute
between Britain and Ireland, would be to side with Britain.

O'CONNOR: You really think his sympathies would have been
with Britain in. . . . He doesn't seem to have had a very
sympathetic reaction when you talked to him about partition,
that's true.

KIERNAN: Well, after all that was the big issue. If your country
is cut in two and that is your major trouble.

O'CONNOR: He didn't show much sympathy at all when you talked with him about it?

KIERNAN: No, he was very cold about it. That is he was looking at it with a cold attitude. You see, Kennedy was in his blood reactions, which after all were completely Irish on both sides, was Irish in his speed of communication, in his wit, in his debunking — self debunking, which is part of the Irish attitude. It's a defensive attitude. In all of that, Irish. Behind that was something that wasn't Irish; the cold summing up, the logical follow up. And in the matters of issues between Ireland and England the reaction might come in a sentimental way. I don't know, but when it came to any kind of practical business, the other man behind, the cold man would take control, which is understandable. And the line I'd draw all the time was one of great understanding, of never any kind of intrusion on him in Irish affairs.

I think his attitude towards Ireland then, was something which grew, which wasn't there at the beginning, because he wanted above all things to be a good New Englander. And when he was in London when his father was Ambassador, he did come across to Ireland and stayed here with David Grey at the Legation as it was then. But he came very much as an English American with English people. He did go to Wexford, but it was rather in the way of "Let's have a look," you know, "I'd like to see what the old sod is like," and so on. The turning point did come on his visit to Ireland. I doubt it came very much before that. It was coming, but when I was in the helicopter with him on the way from Dublin to Galway, he was constantly asking about places. We were low enough to see large-sized houses. He was costing houses. How much would a place like that cost with a certain amount of land attached? I assumed he was wondering just what it would be like to live in Ireland or to have a pied a terre where he could come or send the children occasionally, and so on. One could almost see an affection for Ireland growing out of that visit. I wasn't able to see it before that. He had a sort of an affection or friendship for me because — perhaps because I didn't bother him too much, because we reacted well together, but there was nothing specially pro-Irish. . . .

Document 12 — *Correspondence between Terence O'Neill, Prime Minister of Northern Ireland, and JFK*

NATIONAL SECURITY FILES, BOX 118, KENNEDY LIBRARY

Personal   6th May, 1963

Stormont Castle
Belfast, 4

Dear Mr. President

I would just like you to know how much I appreciated your personal message about the Giant's Causeway handed over to me yesterday by the Consul General in Belfast.

It was with some care that I chose the Giant's Causeway as a possible stopping place. Firstly in 1962 President Eisenhower after a European Tour visited Dublin, but stopped on his way to Belfast. Secondly I realised that a visit to either the NATO communications centre at Londonderry or the American Hall of Remembrance (part of the Northern Ireland War Memorial to be opened by the Queen Mother later this year and attended we hope by Ambassador Bruce) would be embarrassing to your Southern hosts. Thirdly there is a widespread rumour that you visited Portrush before the war when your father was Ambassador in London.

As you know, this part of the world's chief contribution to America was the Scotch-Irish heritage. We proudly claim some 12 American Presidents of this descent. I am busy at the moment seeing if we cannot preserve the Presidential Homes where they are still in existence. At the moment we have located President Arthur's Home in Cullenbackey, Co. Antrim, and President Wilson's at Strabane, Co Tyrone, in the latter the Wilson family are still resident. Moreover, Strabane was also the home of John Dunlap, who printed the Declaration of Independence, and we are marking his home with a plaque. Incidentally there is still in existence an old printing works in this small country town where it is thought that both Wilson and Dunlap served their apprenticeship. In a different sphere of American achievement, all that is left of General Jackson's Home is a stonewall!

Hitherto the closest I have got to the White House has been my annual visits to the I.M.F. Meeting at which I heard you speaking last September. I have also had the pleasure of sitting next to Mrs. Kennedy's mother at a dinner in Vienna at the previous Meeting of the I.M.F. given by Sir William Iliff who was then Vice President to Mr. Eugene Black. I have often thought of sending to Mrs. Kennedy photographs of these Presidential Homesteads after they have been restored and furnished to add to her historical collection now going on at the White House. Perhaps when Lord Antrim and the National Trust in Northern Ireland, of which he is Chairman, have completed this operation I could in fact carry this out.

I would like to end with the following story. Some three years ago I addressed the Philadelphia Scotch-Irish Association. On that occasion an old gentleman gave me a long list of Scotch-Irish millionaires ending with one of your father's predecessors at the Court of St. James — Ambassador Mellon. He added for good measure 'Do you know what! The Scotch-Irish own America and the Southern Irish run it.' I would point out that this was previous to your inauguration!

Once again many thanks for seeing that I got prior knowledge of the message you sent to London. This was a most thoughtful act in the midst of your busy life.

Yours sincerely,
Terence O'Neill

May 13, 1963

The White House
Washington, D.C.

Dear Mr. Prime Minister

Thank you for your thoughtful personal letter of May 6th, and for the spirit in which you have accepted my message about the Giant's Causeway. I fully understand the personal warmth of your nation, and I am genuinely sorry that my schedule simply leaves no room for this stop in June.

I am much interested to know of your efforts in behalf of homes of American Presidents of Scotch-Irish descent, and I am sure that Mrs. Kennedy would enjoy having the photographs of which you speak.

I hardly dare to comment on your amusing story about the relationship between the Scotch-Irish and the Southern Irish in the United States because it would seem unwise to transfer arguments about the ownership of Ireland to the larger area of this country, but I will say that we take pride in all the good Americans that have come out of all parts of Ireland and are grateful to you for your interest in this relationship.

The next time you come to Washington, I hope you will let me know so that we can meet and have a talk. Meanwhile, I thank you again for your friendly letter.

Sincerely,

John F. Kennedy

Document 13 — *Frank D'Arcy, 'The Man Who We Welcome'.* Irish Independent, *26 June 1963*

The most important thing about the man who is arriving in Dublin today is that he is President of the United States. John F. Kennedy, at 46, is not just an American of Irish ancestry who has made a great name for himself. He is first and foremost the American whom his countrymen have chosen to carry responsibilities that affect the rest of mankind.

The President's visit is not only an Irish occasion, but a very American one. The Americans, from the Pilgrim Fathers to the last plane-load from Puerto Rico, are an immigrant people. They are intensely proud of the United States and its life, but they are also to a large degree conscious of origins.

Every year pilgrimages are made to Stratford on Avon or to the house of the Pilgrim Fathers at Leiden in Holland. But the young President's pilgrimage is to a place historic only to Irishmen; or rather, that was historic only to us, for the old farmhouse in Wexford is now part of American history.

When the President stops at Dunganstown, he in fact will draw attention to the end of an era. His great grandfather left this land, like millions of others,

in flight out of misery. They found in America a refuge, but a tough one. They did not become absorbed without trace into their new community. They found that their name, their face and their religion were held against them.

But they in turn mostly decided to hold on to all three: and to stick together until better times. The result took a long time to become clear, but it is clear now when a man can be a Kennedy, a Catholic, with relations in Wexford, and yet be nothing less than a hundred per cent American. The Famine immigrants entered a new society, and were changed by it — and ultimately made some major changes themselves.

The President Kennedy who will step off the plane this evening is a man who has come at the end of this process. Most Irish people already know more about his family background than they do about our own political figures here. They know about his grandfathers who broke into politics, particularly 'Honey Fitz', the singing Mayor of Boston.

They know about his own father, the millionaire who became Ambassador to Britain and who reared an extraordinary family of nine. To avoid knowing and hearing about the good-looking Kennedys, one would have to be a recluse. The President's own wife and family have been under the glare normally reserved for royalty and film-stars.

Modern publicity has also made folklore of the President's exploit in the war — almost twenty years ago — when he obstinately rescued the crew of his sinking torpedo boat. His flat, hard voice has become familiar too, especially from times when the world had good reason to listen to it, as in the midnight broadcast last October when we wondered if the world would go to war over Cuba.

Yet the very barrage of publicity makes it difficult to know what the President is really like, or perhaps more truthfully, it makes it easier to settle for an image that suits each person's preferences. President Kennedy has given no signs of being a nostalgic Boston Irishman. He was reared amid wealth and an involvement in public affairs that were far removed from Boston and the special problems of immigrants.

He has shown himself an American of his own generation. From his early days as a Congressman he became engrossed in the domestic problems that affected the whole of the United States. He showed a passion for analysis, for sounding expert opinion, for weighing up political pressures, and for taking moderate positions.

Ever since he wrote a bestselling book about Europe, at the age of 23, he continued a genuine interest in history, and a certain sense of history. That was clear from his later writings, and from his more notable speeches as President. It could even be that his apparently avid reading of history is the immediate cause of his present visit to Ireland.

The recent notable books presumably attracted his interest — *The Great Hunger* of Cecil Woodham-Smith and a novel which is really a history of the Boston Irish — *The Edge of Sadness* — by Edwin O'Connor. Both these books made one think of the evolution from thatched cottage to White House.

Yet this sense of history is now directed to broader themes. Twice recently he has made major speeches of policy on matters on which he himself will be judged by history. He made a reasoned plea for a new approach to coexistence with the Soviet world, a plea that echoed Pope John's 'Pacem in Terris'. And he has put his Civil

Rights proposals to Congress in an effort to solve the problem of the status of the Negro in the United States.

On his success in dealing with the Russians the peace of the world greatly depends: on his success with Civil Rights — a matter on which he has been criticised for over-caution — depends a great deal of internal American peace. And he faces the dilemma that if he vigorously follows out his liberal principles on civil rights, he might compromise his chances in next year's presidential election by alienating Southern Democrats.

Such preoccupations — and others about the state of his European allies — will surely slip back into his mind as he receives the freedom of our cities and the honours of our statesmen and scholars. But not too much, one hopes, for his visit is a joint Irish and American celebration. He can be reasonably sure, too, that for the next four days he has a nation behind him to a man.

Document 14 — *President Eamon de Valera's welcoming statement, 26 June 1963.* Irish Press, *27 June 1963*

A Uachtarain Uasail in ainm mhuintir na hEireann uile agus thar a gceann cuirim cead mile failte romhat. Cuireann do theacht go hEireann aoibhneas ar chrol gach duine againn agus taimid buioch diot.

[Mr. President, in the name of the people of Ireland and on their behalf, I extend a hundred thousand welcomes. Your coming to Ireland gladdens the heart of everybody and we are very grateful to you.]

Mr. President, I had thought it fitting that my first words of welcome to you should be in our native language, the language of your ancestors, the language that was spoken by the great clan of Dal gCais under their mighty King Brian, nine and a half centuries ago, not far from the spot on which we are standing, crushed the invader and broke the Norse power for ever.

Our welcome, Mr. President, is universal and heartfelt. We welcome you in the first place as the head and chief executive and first citizen of that great Republic of the West upon whose enlightened wise and firm leadership hangs the hope of the world.

We welcome you in the second place as the representative of that great country in which people sought refuge when driven by tyrant laws from their motherland, sought refuge and found themselves and their descendants a home in which they prospered, won renown and gave distinguished service in return.

Finally we welcome you for yourself, as a distinguished son who has won the first place among his countrymen, first in a nation of 180,000,000 people.

We are proud of you here, Mr. President; we admire you for the leadership you are giving and we trust that, under God's inspiration and with His help, you will be able to accomplish the aims which you have in mind, the aims of all who love mankind.

We wish God's blessing upon you and your work.

Document 15 — *JFK statement at New Ross, County Wexford*

ANON., *A MEMORY OF JOHN FITZGERALD KENNEDY; VISIT TO IRELAND, 26TH–29TH JUNE 1963.* (WOOD PRINT, 1963)

Mr. Chairman, I first of all would like to introduce two members of my family who came here with us. My sister Eunice Shriver, and to introduce another of my sisters, Jean Smith. And I would like to have you meet American Ambassador McCloskey, who is with us, and I would like to have you meet the head of the American labour movement, whose mother and father were born in Ireland, George Meany, who is travelling with us. And then I would like to have you meet the only man with us who doesn't have a drop of Irish blood, but who is dying to, the head of protocol of the United States, Angier Biddle Duke.

See, Angie, how nice it is, just to be Irish.

I am glad to be here. It took 115 years to make this trip, and 6000 miles, and three generations. And I am proud to be here and I appreciate the warm welcome you gave to all of us. When my great grandfather left here to become a cooper in East Boston, he carried nothing with him except two things: a strong religious faith and a strong desire for liberty. I am glad to say that all of his great grand children have valued that heritage.

If he hadn't left, I would be working over at the Albatross Company, or perhaps for John V. Kelly. In any case, we are happy to be back here.

About fifty years ago, an Irishman, from New Ross, travelled down to Washington with his family, and in order to show his neighbours how well he was doing, he had his picture taken in front of the White House, and said, 'This is our Summer home. Come and see it.' Well, this is our home also in the winter, and I hope you will come and see us.

Thank you.

Document 16 — *JFK Statement at Cork* — *extract*. Cork Examiner, *29 June 1963*

I come to this island which has been identified with that effort [of national freedom] for a thousand years, which was the first country to lead what was the most powerful tide in the twentieth century, the desire for national independence, the desire to be free, and I come here in 1963 and find that the tide still beating, still runs. . . .

So Ireland is still 'old Ireland', but it has found a new mission in the 1960s, and that is to lead the free world, to join with other countries in the free world, to do in the 1960s what Ireland did in the early part of this century and indeed has done for the last 800 years, and that is associate itself intimately with the principles of freedom.

Document 17 — *Introduction of An Ceann Comhairle, Patrick Hogan, and JFK address to Oireachtas*

COMHSHUI AG DAIL EIREANN AGUS SENAD EIREANN AR OCAID CHHUAIRT, JOHN FITZGERALD KENNEDY. . . . (NATIONAL LIBRARY OF IRELAND, IR. 32841 03)

An Ceann Comhairle:

Mr. President, it is indeed a great honour to have the privilege as Ceann Comhairle of Dail Eireann of welcoming you on behalf of my colleagues and myself to the Parliament of Ireland. For generations the people of Ireland and the people of the United States of America have been closely and intimately associated in times of trial and in times of triumph. The emigrants from our shores have tasted the sweet air of freedom and opportunity sweeping across the broad plains of that hospitable land, and we are proud — very proud indeed — to know that these emigrants were effective and potent factors in the development of that great country. Thus in ordinary circumstances it would be an occasion of pride and privilege for any Irishman to welcome the President of the United States of America to an Irish parliament. But, Mr. President, this is not an ordinary occasion. Your great personality elevates it far above that level. It is an occasion unique as an event in Irish history — it is an international gesture of kindness and goodwill of inestimable value. When the citizen who presides over the great American people of the United States shares with the people of Ireland the heritage of blood, of name and tradition, then the event is enhanced almost beyond measure. May I therefore hasten to extend to you, Mr. President, on behalf of my colleagues and myself a sincere and hearty welcome to the Parliament of Ireland and I respectfully request you to address your eager audience.

Address by President Kennedy:

Mr. Speaker, Prime Minister, Members of the Parliament: I am grateful for your welcome and for that of your countrymen.

The 13th Day of December, 1862, will be a day long remembered in American history. At Fredericksburg, Virginia, thousands of men fought and died on one of the bloodiest battlefields of the American Civil War. One of the most brilliant stories of that day was written by a band of 1,200 men who went into battle wearing a green sprig in their hats. They bore a proud heritage and a special courage, given to those who had long fought for the cause of freedom. I am referring, of course, to the Irish Brigade. As General Robert E. Lee, the great military leader of the Southern Confederate forces, was reported to have said of this group of men after the battle: 'The gallant stand which this bold brigade made on the heights of Fredericksburg is well known. Never were men so brave. They ennobled their race by their splendid gallantry on that desperate occasion. Their brilliant, though hopeless assaults on our lines excited the hearty applause of our officers and soldiers.'

Of the 1,200 men who took part in that assault, 280 survived the battle. The Irish Brigade was led into battle on that occasion by Brigadier General Thomas F. Meagher, who had participated in the unsuccessful Irish uprising of 1848, was captured by the British and sent in a prison ship to Australia, from whence he finally came to America. In the fall of 1862, after serving with distinction and gallantry in some of the toughest fighting of this most bloody struggle, the Irish Brigade was presented with a new set of flags. In the city ceremony, the city chamberlain gave them the motto 'The Union, Our Country and Ireland Forever'. Their old ones having been torn to shreds by bullets in previous battles, Captain Richard McGee took possession of these flags on September 2nd in New York City and arrived with them at the Battle of Fredericksburg and carried them into the battle. Today, in recognition of what these gallant Irishmen and what millions of other Irish have done for my country, and through the generosity of the Fighting 69th, I would like to present one of these flags to the people of Ireland.

[The President then unveiled the flag which was in position to the left of the dais.]

As you can see, gentlemen, the battle honours of the Brigade include Fredericksburg, Chancellorsville, Yorktown, Fair Oaks, Gaines Hill, Allen's Farm, Savage's Station, White Oaks Bridge,

Glendale, Malvern Hills, Antietam, Gettysburg and Bristoe's Station.

I am deeply honoured to be your quest in the free Parliament of a free Ireland. If this nation had achieved its present political and economic stature a century or so ago, my great grandfather might never have left New Ross, and I might, if fortunate, be sitting down there with you. Of course, if your own President had never left Brooklyn, he might be standing up here instead of me.

This elegant building, as you know, was once the property of the Fitzgerald family, but I have not come here to claim it. Of all the new relations I have discovered on this trip, I regret to say that no one has yet found any link between me and a great Irish patriot, Lord Edward Fitzgerald. Lord Edward, however, did not like to stay here in his family home 'because,' as he wrote his mother, 'Leinster House does not inspire the brightest ideas.' That was a long time ago, however. It has also been said by some that a few of the features of this stately mansion served to inspire similar features in the White House in Washington. Whether this is true or not, I know that the White House was designed by James Hoban, a noted Irish-American architect, and I have no doubt that he believed, by incorporating several features of the Dublin style, he would make it more homelike for any President of Irish descent. It was a long wait, but I appreciate his efforts.

There is also an unconfirmed rumour that Hoban was never fully paid for his work on the White House. If this proves to be true, I will speak to our Secretary of the Treasury about it, although I fear this body is not particularly interested in the subject of revenue.

I am proud to be the first American President to visit Ireland during his term of office, proud to be addressing this distinguished assembly and proud of the welcome you have given me. My presence and your welcome, however, only symbolise the many and enduring links which have bound the Irish and the Americans since the earliest days.

Benjamin Franklin, the envoy of the American Revolution, who was also born in Boston, was received by the Irish Parliament in 1772. It was neither independent nor free from discrimination at the time, but Franklyn reported its members 'disposed to be friends of America'. 'By joining our interest with theirs', he said, 'a more equitable treatment . . . might be obtained for both nations'.

Our interests have been joined ever since. Franklin sent leaflets to Irish freedom fighters. O'Connell was influenced by Washington, and Emmet influenced Lincoln. Irish volunteers played so predominant a role in the American Army that Lord Mountjoy lamented in the British Parliament: 'We have lost America through the Irish.' John Barry, whose statue was honoured yesterday, and whose sword is in my office, was only one who fought for liberty in America to set an example for liberty in Ireland. Yesterday was the 117th anniversary of the birth of Charles Stewart Parnell — whose grandfather fought under Barry and whose mother was born in America — and who, at the age of 34, was invited to address the American Congress on the cause of Irish freedom. 'I have seen since I have been in this country,' he said, 'so many tokens of the good wishes of the American people towards Ireland . . .'. And today, 83 years later, I can say to you that I have seen in this country so many tokens of good wishes of the Irish people towards America.

And so it is that our two nations, divided by distance, have been united by history. No people ever believed more deeply in the cause of Irish freedom than the people of the United States. And no country contributed more to building my own than your sons and daughters. They came to our shores in a mixture of hope and agony, and I would not underrate the difficulties of their course once they arrived in the United States. They left behind hearts, fields, and a nation yearning to be free. It is no wonder that James Joyce described the Atlantic as a bowel of bitter tears, and an earlier poet wrote: 'They are going, going, going and we cannot bid them stay'.

But today this is no longer the country of hunger and famine that those immigrants left behind. It is not rich and its progress is not yet complete, but it is, according to statistics, one of the best fed countries in the world. Nor is it any longer a country of persecution, political or religious. It is a free country, and that is why any American feels at home.

There are those who regard history of past strife and exile as better forgotten, but to use the phrase of Yeats: 'Let us not casually reduce that great past to a trouble of fools, for we need not feel the bitterness of the past to discover its meaning for the present and the future.'

And it is the present and future of Ireland that today hold so much promise to my nation as well as to yours, and, indeed, to all mankind, for the Ireland of 1963, one of the youngest of nations, and the oldest of civilizations, has discovered that the achievement of nationhood is not an end, but a beginning. In the years since independence, you have undergone a new and peaceful revolution, an economic and industrial revolution, transforming the face of this land, while still holding to the old spiritual and cultural values. You have modernised your economy, harnessed your rivers, diversified your industry, liberalised your trade, electrified your farms, accelerated your rate of growth and improved the living standard of your people.

Other nations of the world in whom Ireland has long invested her people and her children are now investing their capital as well as their vacations here in Ireland. This revolution is not yet over, nor will it be, I am sure, until a fully modern Irish economy fully shares in world prosperity. But prosperity is not enough.

One hundred and eighty-three years ago, Henry Grattan, demanding the more independent Irish Parliament that would always bear his name, denounced those who were satisfied merely by new grants of economic opportunity. 'A country,' he said, 'enlightened as Ireland, chartered as Ireland, armed as Ireland, and injured as Ireland, will not be satisfied with anything less than liberty.' And, today, I am certain, free Ireland, a full-fledged member of the world community where some are not yet free and where some counsel an acceptance of tyranny — free Ireland will not be satisfied with anything less than liberty.

I am glad, therefore, that Ireland is moving in the mainstream of current world events. For I sincerely believe that your future is as promising as your past is proud, and that your destiny lies not as a peaceful island in a sea of troubles, but as a maker and shaper of world peace.

For self-determination can no longer mean isolation; and the achievement of national independence today means withdrawal from the old status only to return to the world scene with a new one. New nations can build with their former governing powers the same kind of fruitful relationship that Ireland has established with Great Britain — a relationship founded on equality and mutual interests. And no nation, large or small, can be indifferent to the fate of others, near or far. Modern economics, weapons and communications have made us realise more than ever that we are one human family and this one planet is our home. 'The world is large', wrote John Boyle O'Reilly, 'The world is large when its weary leagues two loving hearts divide, but the world is small when your enemy is loose on the other side.'

The world is even smaller today, though the enemy of John Boyle O'Reilly is no longer a hostile power. Indeed, across the gulfs and barriers that now divide us, we must remember that there are no permanent enemies. Hostility today is a fact, but it is not a ruling law. The supreme reality of our time is our indivisibility as children of God and our common vulnerability on this planet.

Some may say that all this means little to Ireland. In an age when 'history moves with the tramp of earthquake feet', in an age when a handful of men and nations have the power literally to devastate mankind, in an age when the needs of developing nations are so large and staggering that even the richest nations often groan with the burden of assistance — in such an age, it may be asked, how can a nation as small as Ireland play much of a role on the world stage?

I would remind those who ask that question, including those in other small countries, of these words of one of the great orators of the English language: ' All the world owes much to the little "five feet high" nations. The greatest art of the world was the work of little nations. The most enduring literature of the world came from little nations. The heroic deeds that thrill humanity through generations were the deeds of little nations fighting for their freedom. And, yes, the salvation of mankind came through a little nation.'

Ireland has already set an example and a standard for other small nations to follow. This have never been a rich or powerful country, and, yet, since earliest times, its influence on the world has been rich and powerful. No larger nation did more to keep Christianity and Western culture alive in their darkest centuries. No larger nation did more to spark the cause of American independence, and independence, indeed, around the world. And no larger nation has ever provided the world with more literary and artistic genius.

This is an extraordinary country. George Bernard Shaw, speaking as an Irishman, summed up an approach to life: 'Other peoples', he said, ' see things and say: 'Why?. . . . But I dream things that never were — and I say: 'Why not?'.

It is that quality of the Irish, the remarkable combination of hope, confidence and imagination that is needed more than ever today. The problems of the world cannot possibly be solved by sceptics or cynics whose horizons are limited by the obvious realities. We need men who can dream of things that never were, and ask why not. It matters not how small a nation is that seeks world peace and freedom, for, to paraphrase a citizen of my country: 'The humblest nation of all the world, when clad in the armour of a righteous cause, is stronger than all the hosts of error.'

Ireland is clad in the cause of national and human liberty with peace. To the extent that the peace is disturbed by conflict between the former colonial powers and the new and developing nations, Ireland's role is unique. For every new nation knows that Ireland was the first of the small countries in the 20th century to win its struggle for independence, and that the Irish have traditionally sent their doctors and technicians and soldiers and priests to help other lands to keep their liberty alive. At the same time, Ireland is part of Europe, progressing in the context of Europe, and a prospective member of an expanded European Common Market. Thus Ireland has excellent relations with both the new and the old, the confidence of both sides and an opportunity to act where the actions of greater powers might be looked upon with suspicion.

The central issue of freedom, however, is between those who believe in self-determination and those in the East who would impose upon others the harsh and oppressive Communist system; and here your nation wisely rejects the role of a go-between or a mediator. Ireland pursues an independent course in foreign policy, but it is not neutral between liberty and tyranny and never will be.

For knowing the meaning of foreign domination, Ireland is the example and inspiration to those enduring endless years of oppression. It was fitting and appropriate that this nation played a leading role in censuring the suppression of the Hungarian Revolution, for how many times was Ireland's quest for freedom suppressed only to have that quest renewed by the succeeding generation? Those who suffer beyond that wall I saw on Wednesday in Berlin must not despair of their future. Let them

*remember the constancy, the faith, the endurance and the final
success of the Irish. And let them remember, as I heard sung by
your sons and daughters yesterday in Wexford, the words: 'The
boys of Wexford, who fought with heart and hand, to burst in
twain the galling chain and free our native land.'*

*The major forum for your nation's greater role in world affairs
is that of protector of the weak and voice of the small, the United
Nations. From Cork to the Congo, from Galway to the Gaza
Strip, from this legislative assembly to the United Nations,
Ireland is sending its most talented men to do the world's most
important work — the work of peace. In a sense, this export of
talent is in keeping with an historic Irish role. But you no longer
go as exiles and emigrants but for the service of your country
and, indeed, of all men. Like the Irish missionaries of medieval
days, like the Wild Geese after the Battle of the Boyne, you are
not content to sit by your fireside while others are in need of
your help. Nor are you content with the recollections of the past
when you face the responsibilities of the present.*

*Twenty-six sons of Ireland have died in the Congo; many
others have been wounded. I pay tribute to them and to all of
you for your commitment and dedication to world order. And
their sacrifice reminds us all that we must not falter now.*

*The United Nations must be fully and fairly financed; its peace-
keeping machinery must be strengthened; its institutions must
be developed until some day, and perhaps some distant day, a
world of law is achieved.*

*Ireland's influence in the United Nations is far greater than
your relative size. You have not hesitated to take the lead on such
sensitive issues as the Kashmir dispute, and you have sponsored
that most vital resolution, adopted by the General Assembly,
which opposed the spread of nuclear arms to any nation not
now possessing them, urging an international agreement with
inspection and control, and I pledge to you that the United
States of America will do all in its power to achieve such an
agreement and fulfill your resolution.*

*I speak of these matters today not because Ireland is unaware
of its role, but I think it important that you know that we know
what you have done, and I speak to remind the other small
nations that they, too, can and must help build a world peace.
They, too, as we all are, are dependent on the United Nations for*

security, for an equal chance to be heard, for progress towards a world made safe for diversity. The peace-keeping machinery of the United Nations cannot work without the help of the smaller nations, nations whose forces threaten no one and whose forces can thus help create a world in which no nation is threatened.

Great powers have responsibilities and their burdens, but the smaller nations of the world must fulfil their obligations as well. A great Irish poet once wrote: 'I believe profoundly in the future of Ireland, that this is an isle of destiny, that that destiny will be glorious, and that when our hour has come we will have something to give to the world.'

My friends, Ireland's hour has come. You have something to give to the world, and that is a future of peace with freedom. Thank you.

Document 18 — *JFK statement at Galway, 29 June 1963.*

*M*r. Mayor, members of the City Council, Prime Minister, Ambassadors. If the day was clear enough and if you went down to the Bay and you looked west and your sight was good enough you would see Boston, Massachusetts.

And if you did, you would see down working on the docks there the O'Dohertys, Flahertys and Ryans, and cousins of yours who have gone to Boston and made good. I wonder if you could, perhaps, let me know how many of you here have relations in America, whom you'd admit to? If you hold up your hands.

I don't know what it is about you that causes me to think that nearly everybody in Boston comes from Galway. They are not shy about it, at all. I want to express as we are about to leave here, to tell you in this country how much this visit has meant.

It is strange that so many years could pass and so many generations pass and still some of us who came on this trip could come home here to Ireland and feel ourselves at home and not feel ourselves in a strange country but feel ourselves among neighbours even though we are separated by generations, by time and thousands of miles.

So you have made all of us. You send us home covered with gifts which we can barely carry, but most of all, most of all, you send us home with warmest memories of you and of your country.

So I must say that although other days be not so bright as we look to the future, that the brightest days will continue to be those on which we visited you here in Ireland.

If you ever come to America, come to Washington, and tell them if they wonder who you are at the gate that you come from Galway. The word will be out and when you do, it will be 'Cead Mile Failte', which means in Gaelic 'A Hundred Thousand Welcomes'.

Document 19 — *Introduction by Lady Mayoress Frances Condell and statement by JFK, Limerick 29 June 1963*

JFK Visit to Ireland; Complete Texts of Addresses

Lady Mayoress Frances Condell:

*M*r. *President, Your Excellency, My Lord Bishop, My Lord Abbot, Very Reverend and Reverend Sirs, Mr. Parliamentary Secretary, Aldermen, Councillors, Honoured Guests, Ladies and Gentlemen.*

Mr. President, I wonder if it is possible for you to realize the great privilege and honour it is for me, and on behalf of my fellow Councillors, Citizens and all those present here this afternoon, to welcome you to our city and county of Limerick. Mr. President, your unexpected but sincerely hoped for decision to come to Limerick was acclaimed with the widest jubilation, and we thank you warmly, Sir, for changing your plans at the last moment to permit us this privilege and joy of meeting you and the other members of your party.

Sir, I am well aware that his Excellency, your ambassador, Mr. McCloskey played a very important and effective part in your granting us this honour. I wish to thank Mr. McCloskey for his understanding and patient bearing with me in allowing me to use him as an ambassadorial pin cushion, whom I kept on prodding to renew our request, of him to the White House, that you come to visit us, Sir. Is it any wonder that the dear man eventually said in exasperation, heaven protect me from a persistent woman. However, I hope that your ambassador has forgiven me by this time, and that you understand with him, Sir, that our enthusiasm to have you come to Limerick was set alight and fanned by a true Irish wind of affection and admiration blowing across the Atlantic to you, with a force of great hereditary pride which we have in the leadership you are displaying, and in your endeavours to accomplish the aims, so dear to all Irish hearts at home and abroad. Mr. President, while listening in awed admiration to your speeches in Germany on Wednesday last and later upon your arrival in Dublin, my mind was directed towards your three-fold headings which you have given as your reason for your work, and your visit to Europe. We, in Ireland, owe much to the three-fold reasoning of another man, who returned to Ireland to give us a faith and a freedom of mind, for which you and we, Sir, are proud to.continue fighting and to· practice in our lives. I refer, of course, to our beloved Irish Saint Patrick, and to the legend of the shamrock with its three leaves growing from one stem. As I listened to you, Mr. President, I could not but interpret your reasoning to a modern idea based on the symbol of the shamrock, and our Christian belief, that you and your people with us, see three good reasons for good living, for determined unity and for working together towards world peace. Three good reasons springing from our common hereditary stem, which inspires towards your aims and the aims of all free people, which we hope you will achieve, Sir, as Saint Patrick did in the name of God. In welcoming you here this afternoon on this race course, Mr. President, I would like you to know, however, that we of Limerick have a lovely city, away in there, beyond the trees and the hills. A city of which we are very proud, steeped as it is in history and antiquity with its charter and its first mayor, reaching away back to the year 1197. It was from our docks, Mr. President, that many emigrant ships set sail for your shores, and from which point of departure our people became yours. That time of great exodus is over, thank God, and I am sure you will agree with me that you have enough of us over there to keep you happy, and to assure you of our faithful support at all times. The day has come when the point of departure and arrival has transferred itself from us, some fifteen miles distant, and in keeping with modern times, to an airport. Limerick benefited immeasurably by its close proximity to Shannon Airport, which for the last eighteen years has served as a major international airport, and as a strong connected link between our Old World and your New one. Because of our proximity to an airport, also, we have the pleasure of welcoming each year many of your fellow countrymen and our returning emigrants. Now with the setting up of the industrial estate at Shannon, in which five American firms have established them-selves during the past couple of years, we have seen the intro-duction to Ireland of a new type of American, who is taking his place in our civic and social life, and who is bringing to our people the skills and techniques of industry. We welcome you,

Sir, on their behalf, as we welcome them on your behalf, and we trust that you will use your influence to send many more industrialists like them, not alone to Shannon, but here in our city of Limerick. I assure you that we shall be very pleased to see a concentration of American industry in Limerick, and in its contiguous area just to help us in this 'leveling up and not down' as you so aptly said in Germany. You see, Mr. President, we the women of Limerick and county feel we have a special claim on you: we claim the Fitzgeralds. May I repeat, we claim the Fitzgerald in you, Sir, and we are extremely proud of that heritage. Over there you see a large number of your relatives and connections who have come to greet you on the distaff side. As a matter of fact, there is only one Kennedy amongst them, a man named Padraig, who has actually written a history, an American history, and who quoted and forecasted many years ago that you would become the President of the United States. And these good people have come to show our Limerick claim on you, and by their presence they prove that the Fitzgeralds are proud of their own Rose, and her dynamic father, Honey Fitz, your reputable and thoughtful and most successful grandfather. But in speaking so much of the Fitzgeralds and the Kennedys we must not forget another woman who is dear to our hearts, your lovely wife, Jacqueline. We shall be pleased if you will take back with you over the Atlantic warmest greetings, Irish prayers and thoughts from the mothers of Limerick city and county to her whose gracious motherhood and wifely devotion and help to you has endeared her to us all. We mothers especially, Sir, only excuse you not bringing your charming Jackie with you to Ireland for the excellent reason that she has for staying at home. We women know that however demanding your presidential commitments may be and the urgency for you to move on, we can only interpret part of that haste to your understandable longing to be back home with her again at this time, and we know that she too, with your children, is counting the hours of your return to her.

And now, Mr. President, on behalf of my fellow councillors and citizens, I ask you to accept the honorary freedom of our city of Limerick. In our full recognition of the great honour you have done us in coming to visit us and in support of your distinguished leadership in aims vital, necessary, united and determined, may God bless you and your family. May your work

*for Him have all the blessings that the prayers of the Irish people
ask for Him for you. I ask you, Mr. President, to accept this
scroll and casket which makes you a freeman, and gives you the
freedom of the city of Limerick. In others words, Limerick is
yours.*

President Kennedy:

*M*adame Mayor, clergy, members of the city council,
*fellow citizens of Limerick, I want to express my thanks
and also my admiration for the best speech that I have
heard since I came to Europe. I asked your distinguished ambassador to the United States, Dr. Kiernan, where is he? I said, what
is this county noted for, and he said it is noted for its beautiful
women and its fast horses, and I said 'you say that about every
county', and he said 'no, this is true about this county'. I want
to express my pleasure in seeing the Fitzgeralds — I wonder if
they could stand up. One of them looks just like Grandpa — and
that's a compliment. I wonder, this is the last place, I go to
another country, and then I am going to Italy, and then back
home to the United States. I wonder before I go, if I could find
out how many citizens here have relations in the United States;
do you think you could hold up your hands if you do? Its no
wonder there's so many of them over there. Well, I tell you that
they've been among the best citizens, and they behave themselves
very well; you'd be proud of them and they're proud of you even
though a great many years have passed since most of them left,
they still remain and retain the strongest sentiments and affection
for this country, and I hope that this visit that we've been able to
make on this occasion has reminded them not only of their past,
but also that here in Ireland the words of freedom, the words of
independence, the whole sentiment of a nation is perhaps
stronger than in almost any place in the world. I don't think that
I've passed through a more impressive ceremony than the one I
experienced yesterday in Dublin when I went with the Prime
Minister to put a wreath on the graves of the men who died in
1916. But to some countries and some people, words of freedom
and words of independence, to see your President who played
such a distinguished part, whose life is so tied up in the life of
this island, in this century all this has made the past very real,*

and it has made the President pretty hopeful, so I carry with me as I go the orchestrated sentiments of appreciation to all of you. This is a great country, with a great people, and I know that when I am back in Washington that I can, while I may not see you, I will see you in my mind, and feel all of your good wishes as we all will, in our hearts. Last night someone sang a song which says, the words of which I am sure you know, 'Come back to Erin, mavourneen, mavourneen, come back again to the land of thy birth, come with the shamrock in the Springtime, mavourneen'. This is not the land of my birth, but it is the land for which I hold the greatest affection, and I will certainly come back in the Springtime.

Document 20 — *Patrick O'Donovan on Kennedy visit to Ireland*. The Observer, *London, 30 June 1963*

Kennedy in Ireland gave the sort of pleasure that makes a man smile to himself on the way home. It was a ritual act like lifting a hat to a lady. It was sentimental as a wedding. It was as much fun as a party.

It served no political purpose. It may even harm the President at home, tying on the Irish label and liability still more firmly, presenting a gadabout image when he should be facing his racial problem.

It was a gratuitous act of recognition by the greatest Power on earth. It meant little in the shifting relationships between States. But it was a civilised and beautiful gesture, and such things need no justification. Ireland asks nothing. She gave nothing except a welcome. There was no humility in her pleasure. She was getting her due.

But in Irish history, this was the first wholly satisfactory act of nationhood; all the others, even to the gaining of independence, have been compromises and less than the best that was possible. This, with a Catholic president from the Irish diaspora singing her praises and taking time off from the brutalities of power, was the real thing.

There was a moment on Friday in a day crowded with helicopter dashes, with parliamentary and academic ceremony, that passed almost unnoticed and yet was the climax of the pilgrimage. The President was taken to a cemetery behind an ugly church lost in the mean back streets of Dublin. It is rather like one of those old London graveyards that have suffered a municipal improvement. The worn tombstones have been moved back and made to line the walls like jobseekers. It is a grey, silent, wholly tragic spot. A gold cross is on one wall and on each side in English and Irish a declaration of independence. In front of it, let into the paving-stones, is a strip of grass.

This is the mass grave of the Easter martyrs, tradesmen, minor poets, school teachers, the men in whose death Yeats found the 'terrible beauty'. They were executed for their leadership of the armed insurrection in Dublin in 1916. Their sacred stronghold was the General Post Office. They were shot close by and the British buried them here and the Irish have made a shrine of the place.

The American President stood before the mass grave in the rain and history came round in a great, calm, majestic circle. Yet there was none of the old ugly anger, such as some of the self-exiled Irish hug to their chests and feed with songs and memories of luxurious bitterness. Pointedly no one mentioned in public the subject of partition. The past was proudly accepted; the present celebrated.

Inevitably it is the incidents, the moments when the robe of ceremony slipped to show the naked man, that stand out. There was the marvelous 'Widow Ryan', for so the Irish papers described her, who presided over the 'homecoming' to Dunganstown where the 'Kennedy homestead' stands.

She is a formidable lady in sensible shoes. She is also a second cousin once removed. Utterly unabashed she dispensed tea and a prodigious midday meal of sandwiches, soda bread and cake. Her farmyard had been concreted over. Her outhouse had been suspected of being the original Kennedy home had been so restored as to be almost unusable. Traders sell models of the outhouse with thatch substituted for the present corrugated iron. The local bogwood rosary trade has flourished in her shadow. She was made to move her authoritative midden. She presided splendidly and even the cameramen treated her with the proper respect.

There was the chairman of the Urban District Council in New Ross. The officials were a little nervous how he would behave. He got in his lick against Northern Ireland by giving the President a bit of the Giant's Causeway, which of course is not — yet — a part of the Irish Republic. The public address system failed. 'Some Pressman', he said, 'has trodden on this thing. Now we're in right trouble.' And a great shout of joy went up.

Then there was the garden party in the rain in Phoenix Park. And the Irish nobs behaved just as badly as their English equivalents. A bishop got his purple cape torn off in the rush and a monsignor used with justification a most surprising word.

And then there were the crowds. Patient, well behaved, not at all hysterical. But radiating pleasure. Ireland has never showed herself to better advantage, never demonstrated more clearly her individuality and maturity, and there was not a trace of shamrockery in sight.

Document 21 — *Eamon de Valera — JFK correspondence July–November 1963*

PRESIDENTIAL OFFICE FILES, BOX 118, KENNEDY LIBRARY

Uachtarain na hEireann
Baile Atha Claith

23 July, 1963

Dear Mr. President,

I was somewhat relieved to see by the newspapers that you are being mobbed in the White House gardens as you were here! Well, that is the penalty. Take care, however, that you do not risk being injured.

I am sending you, separately, a copy of the *Resurrection of Hungary* in which, on page thirty three, is the footnote to which I referred in my little dinner talk here.

I have your presents in the study in which I usually receive visitors. They are wonderfully useful as well as elegant, and are admired by all who see them. I am very grateful.

Please give my regards to Mrs. Shriver, Mrs. Smith and the Princess. I hope that Mrs. Kennedy is very well.

With every good wish from us all.

Very sincerely yours,
Eamon de Valera

The White House

October 15, 1963

Dear Mr. President:

I have asked Prime Minister Lemass to carry this letter back to you following our most pleasant talks in Washington. I want you to know of the particular pride and pleasure that the Prime Minister's visit afforded me.

I have fond memories of my four-day visit to Ireland last June. As I mentioned in my farewell telegram to you, 'I will have the memory of this wonderful Irish welcome in my heart always.'

We have tried to make the Prime Minister's schedule as pleasant and as full as possible. As you know, in addition to visiting Washington, he also visited Philadelphia, New York, Boston and Chicago. When the Prime Minister was in Washington, I told him that the schedule was fit only for a veteran campaigner, but that I was sure he would survive it as I survived my visit to Ireland.

I am confident that the Prime Minister's visit, aside from being a most enjoyable one for all concerned, will further strengthen the firm links that bind our two peoples together. I have been most impressed with Ireland's new Economic Expansion Program, which the Prime Minister described to me. I hope that this progressive program will result in expanded trade and investment relations between our two countries.

I also want to take this opportunity to present you with the Washington-Bailey Sword. This is an authentic reproduction of the sword that General Washington wore throughout most of the Revolutionary War. I think this is appropriate, in view of the large number of men from Ireland who bore arms in defense of the United States in our Revolutionary Wars and in succeeding conflicts.

General Washington's last will and testament provided that each of the General's nephews should receive a sword upon the event of his death. The will enjoined that 'these swords are accompanied with an injunction not to unsheath them for the purpose of shedding blood, except it be for self-defense or in defense of their country and its rights; and in the latter case to keep them unsheathed and prefer falling with them in their hands to the relinquishment thereof.' I think the words of General Washington reflect a sense of values which both Irishmen and Americans share in common.

Would you be so kind as to extend my very best wishes to your gracious wife, who taught me the full significance of the Irish word for welcome, 'Failte', during my memorable June visit.

Very truly yours,
John F. Kennedy

7 November 1963

Dear Mr. President,
     I am sure Ambassador McCloskey has already informed
you with what pleasure I received from the Taoiseach, Mr.
Lemass, your wonderful gift of the replica of the Washington-
Baily sword.
     This sword will be a constant national reminder of the
heroic Irishmen who fought in Washington's Army. It is
always with a feeling of pride that I have opened the pages of
Michael J. O'Brien's book and noted the Irish names to be
found in the rosters and muster rolls of the Continental Army,
and a copy of this book will, I hope, be at hand wherever the
sword may be placed.
     The sword in its case is at present in my study, and it is
with pride that I show it to distinguished visitors.
     With grateful thanks and with deepest regard,
                         I am, Mr. President,
                              Very sincerely yours,
                                   Eamon de Valera

Document 22 — *Frank O'Connor article,*
Sunday Independent, *Dublin, 24 Nov. 1963*

John Fitzgerald Kennedy was a miracle. In three different ways he broke through age-old American prejudices against Catholics, against Irishmen and against intellectuals, and you have to have lived in America to realize how strong these prejudices are. Eleven years ago, in the bar of an exclusive Boston club, an old Bostonian said to me, 'Do you know, you're the first educated Irishman I've ever met?'. At that time, the American universities themselves were being crippled by the McCarthy inquisition.

Kennedy was the fine flower of that great university system. The American university took the Irish literary revival and put it fair and square on every arts course, and when we mock at young Americans who come here to study Yeats and Joyce, we are mocking at the very thing that straightened the backs of men like Kennedy, so that they no longer had to go around pretending they had a great-grandmother from Antrim and were really 'Scotch-Irish'.

Kennedy treated with contempt the Scotch-Irish with the same good-natured contempt with which he treated the native Irish who were afraid of James Joyce's name, and he boldly spoke of Joyce in the Dail, where previously Joyce's name had never been heard except on some debate on evil literature.

In his last speech in Texas he quoted brilliantly from a book of mine. He was not the man to be afraid of quoting some Irish writer, whom most of his audience had never heard of. He was leading the Irish in America out of a ghetto of humiliation and pretence and telling them that they were a people with a history and literature as good as the best. He was also leading educated Americans back into the field of Government from which they had been expelled by the distrust of intellectuals.

On Thursday night I was called to the telephone to hear: 'President Kennedy is quoting from some book of yours in San Antonio, Texas'; on Friday night I was called to the telephone to hear: 'President Kennedy is dead.'

I wept, partly for ourselves, who have lost a man that represented not only his own country but ours; partly for America, whose black fate struck it again.

Document 23 — *John Cogley, 'JFK — A Final Word'.*
Commonweal, *8 May 1964*

[JOHN COGLEY (1916–1976) was a leading American Catholic
intellectual and journalist, editor of *Commonweal* and the *Center
Magazine*. He was Kennedy's religion adviser in the presidential
campaign.]

From the beginning I was an
almost scandalously faithful
supporter of John F. Kennedy.
Sometimes it was a source of
personal embarrassment, for I
realized that it looked to others
like a manifestation of tribal
loyalty at its worst. Here was
Kennedy, Irish-American and
Catholic, and here was I, ditto,
and what could be more natural,
etc., etc.

I remember that back in
1959 *Esquire* magazine polled
a certain number of people
about their hopes for the 1960
Presidential winner. I was one
of those polled, and I replied to
all the other queries but left
blank the space for the actual
choice of candidate. Since I
knew the results would be
published I did not want to
name Kennedy because I felt
it might hurt him by suggest-
ing that he was the 'Catholic
candidate'. In replying to the
questions of what I hoped from
a new Administration, though,
it was John F. Kennedy I had
in mind.

There were times when I
wished Kennedy was a Baptist
and the son of Swedish immigrants so I could feel less self-
conscious about the all-out
support I was prepared to give
him. All my life I had written
and spoken against Catholic
clubbiness and 'our own kind'
thinking. Then, when the first
Irish-Catholic President came
along, I found myself his ardent
supporter. It was unsettling.

Still, now, as the Kennedy
years are already fading into
memory, I think I can honestly
say that it was neither his Irish
inheritance nor religious faith
that really won me but a cast
of thought, a characteristic
political approach and certain
personal traits.

For me, the Kennedy appeal
had something to do with intellectuality, though I never
regarded JFK as an 'intellectual'
in the usual sense of the word.
He was, rather, a man of action,
and that was all right with me.
He used ideas but was never
enthralled by them. This meant,

on the one hand, that his Administration was uncommonly friendly to intellectuals, but, on the other hand, it meant that the totally dedicated intellectuals never quite trusted him, probably because they knew instinctively that he never quite trusted them. Their accustomed indifference to the necessary, and sometimes grubby, means to get good things done and their habit of practising politics, by-proclamation was the President's bone of contention. His cool acceptance of the present reality as the starting point for the thousand-mile journey to the future in turn bothered them. Leaps rather than single steps are the only way to advance in the fast-moving age we live in, the intellectuals insisted; and they felt that Kennedy was too concerned with the techniques of politics and not enough with its goals to make such leaps of thought and of leadership.

My sympathies were notoriously with JFK here, even though my associations were much more intimate with the critical intellectuals than with him and his New Frontiersmen. This meant that I found myself defending the President in the area where he was most vulnerable and his critics most just, and again those nearest and dearest to me.

But the tension between the practicing politician and the intellectual strikes me as inevitable, like the perennial helpful struggle between priest and prophet, and it seemed that John F. Kennedy accepted this too as a fact of life and cherished the intellectuals for what they had to offer, while still realizing that in itself intellectuality is not enough for political leadership. This, to me, meant that though he did not identify with the intellectuals, he had the good sense to be, on the whole, for the intellectuals and to accept their contribution for its full worth. I believe he could not have honored them more, nor should he have honored them less.

Then my sympathy for the President had something to do with style, the most enduring of his qualities. It may be true, as one national columnist recently pointed out, that a preference for style over substance is a deadly political weakness. However in Kennedy's case I never thought of style in such terms. The style of Kennedy was the man Kennedy, and, I believe, it had a great deal to do with the substance of his leadership.

The Cuban confrontation, for example, depended mightily on his style. Any suggestion of either unsureness or bellicosity on his part could have been fatal. Making Khrushchev's capitulation possible, saving the loser's face, so to speak, was another exercise of the Kennedy style which proved to have great substantial significance: though the President tested the limits of deterrence, he did not try to test the limits of human perversity.

The Kennedy style, which at first seemed incomprehensible to some otherwise percipient commentators (remember all that silly talk about the 'cold, had-eyed, humorless young man' in early 1960?) did not get across immediately. But, had JFK lived (and how often we find ourselves repeating that phrase!) it would, I believe, have turned into more political, cultural and educational capital with every passing month — and the whole nation would have benefited.

The sudden realization of what this style had affected us as a people, and how we would miss it, accounted, I believe for the phenomenal sense of loss at the time of his death.

Its no use trying to say what I mean by the Kennedy style. Style is not something one can define exactly, or prescribe for another. It is a gift of the gods and JFK had it in abundance. It has something to do with taste, something to do with restraint and control, and something to do, finally, with grace and gallantry. A rich, powerful, maturing and still uncertain nation needs all the example of what one who is so gifted can offer — as we realized when it was suddenly taken from us.

Finally, my loyalty to JFK had a great deal to do with his modernity.

I know there are many reasons why one might think of the present era as a totally undesirable period to live in. No generation of men has been witness to evil on a more colossal scale. None has had to bear with such uncertainty about the very future of the human race. None has had to live with problems so complex and failure to solve them so awesome. But, for all that, Kennedy seemed to say, it is a good time to be alive; maybe even because the challenges appear so stupendous, it is a good time to be alive.

John F. Kennedy communicated this sense of sane *joie de vivre* to the whole world and particularly to the young. Perhaps it was a result of his own comparative youth in a position usually filled by older men, but I don't think so. I think, rather, that it had something to do with his disdain for whimpering; his cool (that word keeps coming back) acceptance of contemporary reality and not because it was contemporary either but because it was presently real; his lack of fear of any idea and unspoken insistence that an idea, after all, is only an idea and not the stuff of life itself; and, finally, his abiding sense of history — the frantic contemporariety which many mistake for modernity did not mar his appreciation of the present. . . .

Document 24 — *'The Boys of Wexford', by Robert Dwyer Joyce*

PRESIDENTIAL OFFICE FILES, BOX 118, KENNEDY LIBRARY

In comes the captain's daughter, the captain of the Yeos,
Saying, 'Brave United man, we'll ne'er again be foes.
A thousand pounds, I'll give you, and fly from home with thee,
And dress myself in man's attire, and fight for libertie!

Refrain:
We are the boys of Wexford, who fought with heart and hand
To burst in twain the galling chains, and free our native land!

I want no gold, my maiden fair, to fly from home with thee;
Your shining eyes will be my prize — more dear than gold to
    me.
I want no gold to nerve my arm to do a true man's part —
To free my land I'd gladly give the red drops from my heart.

Refrain

And when we left our cabins, boys, we left with right good will,
To see our friends and neighbours that were at Vinegar Hill!
A young man from our ranks, a cannon he let go;
He slapt it into Lord Mountjoy — a tyrant he laid low!

Refrain

We bravely fought and conquered at Ross and Wexford town
And if we failed to keep them 'twas drink that brought us down.
We had no drink beside us on Tubberneering's day,
Depending on the long bright pike, and well it worked its way!

Refrain

They came into the country
Our blood to waste and spill; but let them weep for Wexford,
And think of Oulart Hill! 'twas drink that still betrayed us —
Of them we had no fear; for every man could do his part
Like Forth and Shelmalier!

My curse upon all drinking! It made our hearts full sore;
For bravery won each battle, but drink lost evermore.
And if, for want of leaders we lost at Vinegar Hill,
We're ready for another fight, and love our country still!

We are the boys of Wexford, who fought with heart and hand
To burst in twain the galling chains, and free our native land!

REFERENCES

Introduction

1. Kenneth O'Donnell and David Powers (with Joe McCarthy), *'Johnny, We Hardly Knew Ye'*; *Memories of John Fitzgerald Kennedy*, p.367.
2. Andrew Greeley and William C. McCready, *Ethnicity in the United States* — in particular, chapter 4; *Boston Globe*, 18 July 1960.
3. Theodore H. White, *The Making of the President*: 1960, p.172; *ibid.*, *In Search of History; A Personal Adventure*, pp.608–09.
4. Harris poll, *Washington Post*, 1 July 1963; Gallup poll, *ibid.*, 7 July 1963.

Chapter One: Family and Politics

1. Edward Pessen, *The Log Cabin Myth*; *Social Origins of American Presidents*, (Hartford, Conn., 1984).There have been 12 presidents of at least part-Irish ancestry. In 1981 Debretts of London listed nine, but did not include Andrew Johnson (whose mother's name was Mary McDonough) or Harry Truman; since then Bill Clinton (whose mother's maiden name was Cassidy) has become president. *New York Times*, 5 January 1981.
2. *Report of the Committee on Linguistic and National Stocks in the Population of the United States*. American Historical Association, Annual Report: 1931; see also, David N. Doyle, Ireland, *Irishmen and Revolutionary America*, (Dublin, Ireland, 1981).
3. Steven P. Erie, *Rainbows End; Irish-Americans and the Dilemmas of Urban Machine Politics, 1840–1985*, (Berkeley, 1988) chs. pp.1–3; Dáil Éireann, Private Sessions of the Second Dáil, (18 Aug. 1921) p.13.
4. Marjorie Fallows, *Irish-Americans: Identity and Assimilation*, (New York, 1979) pp.125–26; Andrew Greeley, *The Irish Americans;*

The Rise to Money and Power (New York, 1981); Doris Kearns Goodwin, *The Fitzgeralds and the Kennedys*, chs. 1–9.

5. Irish Press,8 July 1938; P.J. as Irish patriot; Maurice Hennessy, *I'll Come Back in the Springtime*, p.11; Richard Whalen, *The Founding Father; The Story of Joseph P.Kennedy*, p.104.

6. Whalen, *Founding Father*, pp.5–7, 104. (Mary Hickey Kennedy, an ambitious, forceful woman, was a powerful influence on her son. She died in 1923, when Jack was six); Burton Hersh, *The Education of Edward Kennedy*, pp.14–16.

7. Doris Kearns Goodwin, *The Fitzgeralds and the Kennedys*, p.159.

8. *Boston Travellers*, 2 August 1947, *Cork Examiner*, 29 June 1963.

9. Nigel Hamilton, *JFK:Reckless Youth*, p.59; Rose Fitzgerald Kennedy, *Times to Remember; An Autobiography*, p.405.

10. Hamilton, *JFK*, p.73; Peter Collier and David Horowitz, *The Kennedys*, pp.44–45.

11. Whalen, *Founding Father*, pp.166, 199–203; Michael R. Beschloss, *Kennedy and Roosevelt: The Uneasy Alliance*, pp.153–57; Hamilton, JFK, pp.97, 108.

12. Lord Longford and T.P. O'Neill, *Eamon de Valera*, (Boston, 1971) p.318; T.P. O'Neill interview, 5 August 1992.

13. David E. Koskoff, *Joseph P. Kennedy: A Life and Times*, p.132.

14. *Ibid.*, pp.133, 142; Longford and O'Neill, *De Valera*, pp.323–24.

15. *Irish Press*, 9 July 1938; Hamilton, *JFK*, 286.

16. *Irish Independent*, 8 July 1938; *Irish Press*, 8 July 1938; Hamilton, *JFK*, p.233.

17. Note by Loretta Kennedy Connelly to JFK, JFK to Connelly, 13 March 1959. JFK Pre-Presidential Papers, Senate — general files, box 527, JFK Library.

18. L. Connelly to JFK, 21 August 1959; Josephine Grennan, oral history transcript, JFK Library.

19. *Irish Press*, 8 July 1938.

20. *New York Times*, 8,9,12 July 1938; Koskoff, 142; *Irish Press*, 9 July 1938; US Minister to Ireland to Joe, 17 January 1946, JFK Private Papers, general correspondnce, box 4a; Ralph G. Martin, *A Hero For Our Times; an Intimate Story of the Kennedy Years*, (New York, 1983) p.38.; David E. Koskoff, *Joseph P. Kennedy: A Life and Times*, p.33.

In January 1941 Kennedy was interested in acting as a mediator between the Irish and British Governments concerning military facilities in Ireland. Besshloss, *Kennedy and Roosevelt*, pp.235, 302.

21. Jean and Clay Blair, Jr., *The Search for JFK*, pp.29–45; Michael J. Rosanova, *A Crisis of Succession: A Multi-Generational Kantorian Systems Analysis of the Kennedy Family, Centering on the Years 1940–48*, Yale Ph.D. dissertation, 1980, pp.112, 156; Rose F. Kennedy, *Times to Remember*, p.405; Joe McCarthy, *The Remarkable Kennedys*, p.74. Noble and Greenough — Hamilton, JFK, pp.53–55.; Groton — Carl M. Brauer, *Kennedy and the Second Reconstruction*, p.13; Hamilton, *JFK*, pp.126, 205; James T. Crown, *The Kennedy Literature; a Bibliographical Essay on JFK*, (New York, 1968) p.25; Harvard — Herbert S. Parmet, *Jack: The Struggles of JFK*, p.43; Martin, Hero, p.241; Kennedy sisters: D.K.Goodwin, *Fitzgeralds and Kennedys*, p.488; William Manchester, *One Brief Shining Moment; Remembering Kennedy*, pp.58, 31.

22. Hugh Fraser, oral history transcripts; David Nunnerly, *Kennedy and Britain*, p. 17.

23. Garry Wills, *The Kennedy Imprisonment: A Meditation on Power*, pp.72–74.

24. JFK to Kathleen K., 10 March 1942, correspondence, 1933–50, box 4a, JFK Personal Papers.

25. Whalen, *Founding Father*, p.170; Rose K. to children, 9 Oct. 1942, correspondence, 1933–50.

26. J.M.Burns, oral history transcript; Kenneth O'Donnell and David Powers, *Johnny*, p.45, 50; Hamilton, *JFK*, pp.286, 380.

27. Hamilton, *JFK*, pp.352–54.

28. *New York Journal American*, 2 February 1941.

29. Blairs, *Search for JFK*, pp.173, 264. 324; Paul B. Fay, Jr., *The Pleasure of His Company*, (New York, 1966), p.146.

30. Blairs, *Search*, p.385; Hamilton, *JFK*, pp.712, 714–16; *New York Journal American*, 29 July 1945.

31. Both Lemuel Billings and Charles Spaulding, two of his closest friends, believed that Jack would have been in politics even if Joe Jr. had lived. Hamilton, *JFK*, pp.673, 689–90, 461, 473.

32. Joseph Dineen, *The Kennedy Family*, 118–24; Doris K. Goodwin, *The Fitzgerald and the Kennedys*, p.708. Joe Kane on Curley— Hamilton, *JFK*, 674, 704; Jack Beatty, *Rascal King*, pp.456–57. Joseph F. Leahy, David Powers, oral history transcripts; William G. Carleton, 'Kennedy in History: an Early Appraisal', in J.B. Walsh, ed., The Irish: America's Political Class, p.282.; JFK 1945 speech — Pre-Presidential Papers, box 94.

33. Lynne McTaggart, *Kathleen Kennedy; Her Life and Times*, pp.210–19;
    Blairs, *Search* pp.557–58.

34. Many years later when interviewed for the Kennedy Library, Pamela
    Churchill said she was 'very impressed' by the dignity of the couple
    she met at Dunganstown. By that time she was the wife of Averill
    Harriman, American millionaire and a leader in the Democratic
    Party. In March 1993 she was appointed US Ambassador to France.
       Blairs, *Search*, p.559; Burns, *Kennedy* pp.3–4; Pamela Digby
    Churchill Harriman oral history transcript; *Boston Traveller*,
    2 August 1947; *Boston Globe*, 10 Sept. 1947; *New Ross Standard*,
    11 November 1960; JFK to L. Connelly, 13 March, 20 August 1959;
    L. Connelly to JFK, 21 August, JFK to J.M.Burns, 25 August
    1959, President's Office Files, Personal Secretary's Files, box 129,
    folder: 'Books-JFK, A Political Profile', Kennedy Library, Boston;
    T.P. Coogan, 'It's County Kennedy Now!', *Irish Digest*, September
    1963; D.K.Goodwin, *Fitzgeralds and Kennedys*, pp.729–32.

35. Frank Moore O'Ferrell oral history transcript. In 1955 Kennedy
    said his last visit had been six years previously. *Irish Independent*, 1
    October 1955.

36. Commonwealth of Massachusetts, *Election Statistics*: 1952, p.5;
    Martin, *Hero*, p.66; Arthur M. Schlesinger, Jr., *Robert Kennedy
    and His Times*, p.97.

37. Frank Aiken, John E. Fogarty oral history transcripts; Ted Reardon
    1952 compilation, JFK Personal Papers, biographical materials,
    box 1; *Congressional Record*, volume 97, part 9, pp.12270–12287,
    27 September 1951; letter to constituent, 22 January 1957, Pre-
    Presidential Papers, Senate files, legislation, 1956–57, box 670
    T.J. Kiernan, oral history transcript.

38. St. Patrick's Day speeches, 1954–57, Senate, speech files, boxes
    894–95; John Wright to JFK, 10 March 1954, ibid., box 894;
    Sorensen, Kennedy, 59; Library of Congress, *John F. Kennedy; a
    Compilation of Statements and Speeches . . . in Senate and
    House of Representatives*, (Washington, D.C., 1964) p.557.

39. Irish-French cultural connection — Michael J. Rosanova, 'Crisis of
    Succession', pp.154–55; Jackie's French ancestors, no mention of
    Irish — *New Yorker*, 15 June 1963; Martin, *Hero*, pp.71, 81; C.
    David Heymann, *A Woman Named Jackie*, pp.17–18; John H. Davis,
    The Bouviers; Portrait of an American Family, pp.257–58; *ibid., The
    Kennedys; Dynasty and Disaster, 1848–1983*, pp.157, 169–171.

40. Herbert Parmet, *Jack: the Struggles of John F. Kennedy*, p.223; Martin, *Hero*, pp.71, 81; Fay, *Pleasure*, p.165; Kitty Kelley, *Jackie Oh!*, pp.36, 44–45.

41. Hennessy, *Springtime*, pp.30–37; Liam Cosgrave oral history transcript; Father Thomas Fagan, All Hallowes College, interview; *Irish Independent*, 1 October 1955.

Chapter Two: The Presidency

1. Doris Kearns Goodwin, *The Fitzgeralds and the Kennedys*, chapter 39; J.M. Burns, JFK, p.181; T. Sorensen, *Kennedy*, pp.91–92.

2. Burton Hersh, *The Education of Edward Kennedy; A Family Biography*, Norton transcript pp.65–66, 86–88, 90–95, 110; Theodore H. White, *The Making of the President 1960*, (New York, 1961), p.283.

3. Joseph Huthmacher, JFK review, 'The Voter's Choice in the Bay State', in *Massachusetts Peoples and Politics, 1919–1930. New York Times Book Review*, 20 September 1959; JFK, *A Nation of Immigrants*, (New York, 1964), pp.17–51, 84.

4. James M. Curley, *I'd Do it Again; a Record of All My Uproarious Years*, (Englewood Cliffs, NJ, 1957); 'A Hurrah for Curley by Curley', *Life* magazine, 10 September. 1956; Joseph Dineen, *The Kennedy Family*, (Boston, 1959), pp.191–92; Jack Beatty, *Rascal King* p.250.

5. T.H. White, *In Search of History*, p.463; O'Donnell and Powers, *Johnny*, p.153.

6. T.H. White, *In Search of History*, p.608 ; O'Donnell and Powers, *Johnny*, p.147; Ralph G. Martin, *A Hero for Our Time*, pp.143, 171. Gene McCarthy, Abigail McCarthy, *Private Faces; Public Places*, pp.221–24; Arthur Herzog, *McCarthy for President*, pp.53–58. Arthur Schlesinger, Jr., *Robert Kennedy and His Times*, p.215.

7. Mark R. Levy and Michael S.Kramer, *The Ethnic Factor; How America's Minorities Decide Elections*, pp.16–17, 125–27, 138.

8. Laurence Fuchs, 'A Catholic as President?', *America*, 13 September. 1958; 'Catholics, Protestants and '60', *Newsweek*, 1 June 1959 MacLeish article in *Life* magazine cited in 'Reality and the American Dream', *Commonweal*, 8 July 1960. See also Victor Lasky, *Robert F. Kennedy; The Man and the Myth*, p.37; Manchester, *Brief Shining Moment*, pp.130–31.

9. National Security files, file no. 118, 24 January, 1961; Andrew J. Minihan, oral history transcript, Kennedy Library; *New Ross Standard*, 27 January, 1961.

10. Laurence Thompson and R. H. Winnock, *Robert Frost; the Later years, 1938–1963*, (New York, 1976) pp.277, 282–83, 287, 304; Nancy Dickerson, *Among Those Present*, p.67; William Manchester, *Portrait of a President*, (New York, 1962) p.72 Manchester later decided that Kennedy had a strong sense of Irish identity. *Brief Shining Moment*, p.55–56); Ralph G. Martin, *Hero*, p.38; 'Editorials: "Harvard 6, Irish 6"', *America*, 9 December 1961.

11. Pierre Salinger, *With Kennedy*, p.64; Dickerson, *Among Those Present*, p.67; White, *1960*, pp.21, 284; O'Donnell and Powers, *Johnny*, pp.235, 293–94; Dave Powers as 'court jester' and friend — Parmet, *JFK*, p.302; Gerald S. and Deborah Strober.eds., *Let Us Begin; An Oral History of the Kennedy Presidency*, (*New York, 1993) pp.142–43*; Louis Martin in Kenneth W. Thompson ed., *The Kennedy Presidency* pp.91–92; B. Bradlee, *Conversations with Kennedy*, pp.190, 233; Fay, *Pleasure*, pp.124–25; George Smathers transcript, Kennedy Library.

12. Thomas J. Kiernan oral history transcript, JFK Library; National Security files box 118; Martin, *Hero*, p.290.

13. National security files, box 118; JFK to Stockdale, 23 October, 3 November 1961, Presidential Office files, box 119a; Kiernan transcript.

14. Edward B. Clafin, ed., *Memos from the President's Office, 1961–63*, p.182; Kiernan oral history transcript.

15. *Ibid*.

16. *Irish Times*, 1 January 1993.

17. Frank Aiken, oral history transcript; T.P.O'Neill interview; 10 August 1992.

18. *Irish Independent*, 25 February 1962; *Irish Times*, 1 January. 1993; James M. Burns, *Edward Kennedy and the Camelot Legacy*, pp.75, 96.

19. McCloskey to S.S., 18 January. 1963, NSF, box 118; Tubridy transcript; Breadlee, *Conversations*, p.192; O'Donnell and Powers, *Johnny*, pp.358–59.

20. Dev to JFK, 27 March 1963, JFK to Msg. Patrick O'Flahery, 27 May 1963, POF, box 119a; O'Donnell and Powers, *Johnny*, p.359; Owen Dudley Edwards article, *Irish Times*, 26 June 1963; J. M. Burns transcript.

21. America Ireland Foundation: *Hibernia*, June 1963; Kiernan to E. Lincoln, 18 June 1963; POF, box 119a; *Irish Times*, 30, 31 August. 1963.

22. L. O'Brien, *No Final Victories*, p.152; Salinger, *With Kennedy*, p.171, T.P.O'Neill interview.

23. O'Neill finally got into the White House — on 17 March, 1964. He was ushered into the Oval Office in the wake of a shouting match between President L.B.Johnson and Senator Mike Mansfield (the subject of which was Vietnam?), had a quick handshake and photo op and was led out by McGeorge Bundy, who expressed regret that O'Neill had not got to meet Kennedy. Terence O'Neill to JFK, 6 May; reply, 15 May; O'Neill to JFK, 16 August; reply, 25 August. 1963, NSF, box 118; T. O'Neill, *The Autobiography of Terence O'Neill*, pp.48–52, 56–59.

24. *Hibernia*, August. 1963; Bradlee, *Conversations*, p.193; Gordon Lieberson ed., Mary Ryan statement in JFK ; O'Donnell and Powers, *Johnny*, A. Minihan transcript; p.362.

25. Jerry Bruno and Jeff Greenfield, *The Advance Man*, p.70; Frank D'Arcy interview; *Irish Independent*, 25 June 1963.

26. O'Donnell and Powers, *Johnny*, p.362.

Chapter Three: Coming Back

1. Paul Bew and Henry Patterson, *Sean Lemass and the Making of Modern Ireland, 1945–1966*, chapters. 4–6; *Irish Independent*, 27 June 1963; E. Lincoln, *My Twelve Years With John F. Kennedy*, p.345.

2. Kiernan transcript; Brian Inglis, 'Kennedy in Ireland', *Spectator*, 5 July 1963; *Cork Examiner*, 27 June 1963; Eamon deValera transcript, Kennedy Library.

3. O'Donnell and Powers, *Johnny*, pp.363–65.

4. Minihan transcript; Bradlee, *Conversations;* Anon., *A Memory of JFK; Visit to Ireland; 26–29 June 1963*, pamphlet; Frank D'Arcy interview; O'Donnell and Powers, *Johnny*, pp.363–64; Tubridy transcript, Kennedy Library.

5. Inglis article; Mary Ryan in Goodard Lieberson, ed., *JFK; As We Remember Him*, p.205; Jim Kennedy statement — *Irish Press*, 28 June 1963. *Irish Independent* 28 June version of his parting words: 'I've got to go. Thanks a lot, dear. I'll be back.' *Irish Times*, 28 July 1963.

6. O'Donnell and Powers, *Johnny*, p.365; *Cork Examiner*, 29 June 1963; *Irish Press*, 28, 29 June 1963.

7. Oireachtas address — Comhshui ag Dáil Éireann agus Seanad Éireann ar ocaid chuairt Seán Fitzgerald Cinneide, Uachtaráin

Stait Aontaithe Mheirice; Inglis article; *Irish Times*, 29 June, 1963; Sean Ó Luing interview.

8. O'Donnell and Powers, *Johnny*, p.368; Lemass oral history transcript.

9. *Johnny*, pp.370–71; Larry O'Brien, *No Final Victories*, p.152; *Irish Times*, 1 July 1963.

10. *Irish Times*, 2 July; *Irish Independent*, 3 July; *Sunday Press*, 30 June 1963; *Hibernia* July 1963.

11. Kiernan transcript.

12. *Irish Independent*, 4 July 1963.

13. David Powers interview.

Chapter Four: After

1. Drew Pearson articles, 2, 6 July 1963, *Washington Post*; O'Brien, *No Final Victories*, p.164.

2. James Reed, Sean Lemass oral history transcripts; Fay, *Pleasure*, p.127; Gallagher, *Life With Jacqueline*, p.277.

3. JFK to Mrs. Dev, 9 July; Dev to JFK, 23 July; JFK to Dev, 19 August 1963. President's Office Files, box 119a.

4. Teacher's visit — Mairin Quill, TD, in *Irish Independent*, 26 June 1993; Lemass transcript; E. Lincoln to M. McCloskey, 26 July 1963; JFK to Fr. T. Kennedy, 19 August. 1963, POF, box 119a, Kennedy Library.

5. Reed, Kiernan oral history transcripts; B. O'Kelly contacted Kennedy, Presidential Papers, Kennedy Library.

6. JFK to Dev, 15 October 1963, National Security Files, box 118; Kiernan, Lemass transcripts; *Irish Independent*, 16, 17 October 23 November. 1963.

7. Reed transcript, Kennedy Library.

8. JFK to Dev, 15 October 1963, National Security Files, box 118.

9. T.H.White, *Making of the President: 1964*, p.24; O'Donnell thought to himself — *Johnny*, p.21.

10. O'Donnell and Powers, *Johnny*, pp.39–40; Josephine Grennan transcript, Kennedy Library; Manchester, *Death of President*, p.645.

11. *Irish Times*, 25 November 1963; *Sunday Independent*, 24 November 1963; *Irish Independent*, 4 December 1963; N. Furlong, The Wexford Guide, Bord Fáilte.

12. Owen V. Mooney, 'The John F. Kennedy memorial park', *Capuchin Annual*, 1974, pp.217–28.

13. *Sunday Press*, Dublin, 20 June 1993.

14. *New York Times*, 14 June–20 July 1967.
15. Ted K — 'Day of joy and sadness', *Saturday Evening Post*, 11 July 1964; James M. Burns, *Edward Kennedy and the Camelot Legacy*, p.181; Hachey, Hernon and McCaffrey, *Irish Experience*, pp.252–53; *Irish Echo*, 2–9 March 1993; Kennedy address to the College Historical Society, Trinity College, Dublin; 'Joint Appeal for Peace in Northern Ireland', Friends of Ireland, 1977; annual statements from Friends, 1981–1993, Edward M. Kennedy office files.
16. Arthur Schlesinger, *Robert Kennedy and His Times*, p.849; Edward M. Levine, *The Irish and Irish Politicians*, pp.159–60.
17. *Boston Globe*, 28 December 1990; *Irish Echo*, 10–16 June 1992, 3–9 March 1993; Francis J. Costello to author, 5 March 1993; JFK press releases, 15 January 24, 26 February 1993.
18. *Irish Times*, 20 March, 26 June 1993; transcript of hearing, nomination of Jean Kennedy Smith, US Senate Committee on Foreign Relations, 9 June 1993; interviews, Kevin O'Byrne and Mariead ni Chiosoig.
19. Kennedy Trust brochure, Sean Reidy interview, *New Ross Echo*, 17 June, 12 August 1993.

Chapter Five: Looking Back

1. T. H. White, *The Making of the President: 1964*, p.25; 'Selective legislative accomplishments of the 86th and 87th Congresses' in T. Sorensen, *Kennedy*, pp.759–60; Donald Lord, *JFK*, p.21; John W. McCormack, oral history transcript, Kennedy Library; Irving Bernstein, *Promises Kept*; *John F. Kennedy's New Frontier* (New York, 1991).
2. Bartlett statement — Kenneth W. Thompson, ed., *The Kennedy Presidency*, p.16; O'Donnell, *Johnny*, pp.13–17; Mansfield — Schlesinger in Thompson, *Kennedy Presidency*, p.31 and letter in *Times Literary Supplement*, 3 April 1992; Hilsman — *ibid*, and *To Move A Nation*, pp.525–37; *New York Times*, 21 November 1983. See also Manchester, *Brief Shining Moment*, pp.313–28.
3. Murray Kempton, 'The Last Big Rally', *New York Post*, 8 November 1960, in *America Comes of Middle Age*, (Boston, 1963) pp.293–96.
4. T.P.O'Neill, *Man of the House: The Life and Political Memoirs of Speaker 'Tip' O'Neill*, (New York, 1979) pp.96–99; McDonough story related to me by bartender, Scituate Country Club, Scituate, Massachusetts, circa 1985.

5. Melbourne — James T. Crown, *Kennedy Literature*, 58; 'After the Anniversary', *Spectator*, 1 December 1964.

6. Muggeridge, 'The Apotheosis of John F. Kennedy', New York Review of Books, 28 January 1965, in Thomas Brown, JFK; *History of an Image*, p.47; Nigel Hamilton, *JFK: Reckless Youth*, pp.97, 108, 209, 693.

7. Manchester, *Portrait of a President*, (New York, 1962) p.72; Sorensen, *A Thousand Days*, p.581; Manchester, *Brief Shining Moment*, pp.55–56.

8. Wills, *Kennedy Imprisonment*, pp.61–67.

9. *Ibid.*, pp.72–75.

10. Ralph Martin, *A Hero for Our Time*, p.38; Manchester, *Portrait*, p.73; David Burner and Thomas R. West, *The Torch is Passed: The Kennedy Brothers and American Liberalism*, (New York, 1984) p.190.

11. Fuchs, *John F. Kennedy and American Catholicism*, pp.210–11.

12. Burner and West, 'Kennedy Liberalism', *Torch is Passed*, pp.150–92. For an earlier period, see John D. Buenker, *Urban Liberalism and Progressive Reform*, (New York, 1973).

13. J.M. Burns oral history transcript, Kennedy Library.

14. Donald C. Lord, *John F. Kennedy*, p.21; Nathan Glazer and Daniel p.Moynihan, *Beyond the Melting Pot*, p.287.

15. Arthur Schlesinger Jr, *Robert Kennedy and His Times*, pp.61–62, 64–65.

16. Rose Kennedy, *Times to Remember*, p.405; Paul Pay, *The Pleasure of His Company*, p.126; Dave Powers in Doris K. Goodwin, *Fitzgeralds and Kennedys*, p.708; Clement A. Norton, John E. Powers, oral history transcripts.

   Nehru-Kennedy exchange: Arthur Schlesinger, *A Thousand Days*, p.525, says that one or two of Nehru's allusions 'especially a bit on Ireland, seemed to me a trifle condescending'. I wonder what he said! According to J. Kenneth Galbraith, *A Life in Our Times*, p.409, Nehru was 'enchanted' by Edwin O'Connor's The Last Hurrah. Dorothy Tubridy — *Irish Times*, 2 December 1963; Thomas N. Brown, 'The Political Irish', in D.N. Doyle and O.D. Edwards, eds., *America and Ireland, 1776–1976*, p.145.

17. T.P. Coogan, *Ireland Since the Rising*, (New York, 1966) pp.181–82; John A. Murphy, *Ireland in the Twentieth Century*, (Dublin, 1975) p.147; F.S.L. Lyons, *Ireland Since the Famine*, (London 1971) p.586; Ronan Fanning, *Independent Ireland*, (Dublin, 1980)

p.203. Fergal Tobin, *The Best of Decades; Ireland in the 1960s*, (Dublin 1984), pp.91, 94; Thomas Hachey, Joseph Hernon and Lawrence McCaffrey, *The Irish Experience*, (Englewood Cliffs, N.J., 1989) pp.227–28. James Downey viewed Kennedy as an American aristocrat, imperialist and a man with an 'arrogant soul'. 'Kennedy and the years of false promise', *Irish Times*, 8 November 1980; Lord Longford believed that Kennedy probably would have become more Irish had he lived. *Kennedy*, (London, 1976) pp.200–01. See also comments Owen Dudley Edwards, 'Conclusion: some counter themes' and Thomas N. Brown, 'The political Irish' in D.N.Doyle and O.D.Edwards, eds., *America and Ireland, 1776–1976* (Greenwood Press, 1980) pp.307–08, 143–46.

18. Joseph J. Lee, *Ireland, 1912–1985; Politics and Society*, (London, 1989) pp.341–58; T.P. O'Neill interview.

19. One of his original campaign aides, Patrick J. 'Patsy' Mulkern has said that after two terms as US President Kennedy would have sought the presidency of Harvard: 'That would have been the next move for him. . . . That's his Irish. He used to tell me that. After that.' Mulkern oral history transcript, Kennedy Library.

BIBLIOGRAPHY

I. Documents
John F. Kennedy Library, Boston
>National Security files
>Personal Correspondence
>Pre-Presidential Files — House of Representatives
>Pre-Presidential Files — Senate
>Presidential Office files

Congressional Record, 1954, 1956, 1957

National Archives of Ireland, Files in connection with President Kennedy's visit to Ireland, June 1963, 434/682, 1–23.

II. Oral History Transcripts
Aiken, Frank
Burns, James M.
Cosgrave, Liam
DeValera, Eamon
Fogarty, John E.
Fraser, Hugh
Grennan, Josephine
Harriman, Pamela Digby Churchill
Kiernan, Thomas J.
Lemass, Sean F.
McCormack, John W.
Minihan, Jeremiah
Smathers, George
Tubridy, Dorothy

III. Material from Kennedy Congressional Offices
1. Sen. Edward M. Kennedy. Press releases, speeches concerning Northern Ireland, 1979–1993.
2. Congressman Joseph P. Kennedy II. Articles, speeches concerning Northern Ireland, 1987–1993.

IV. Interviews
Croke, Jane F.
Daly, Charles U.
D'Arcy, Frank
Fagan, Thomas
Gallagher, Colm
Gerry, Elizabeth A.
Griffin, Joseph M.
Leonard, Helen L.
O'Neill, Thomas P., Dublin
Powers, David
Watson, James R.

V. Bibliographies
BLESSING, Patrick J., *The Irish in America: A Guide to the Literature and Manuscript Collections*. Washington, D.C., 1992.
CROWN, James T., *The Kennedy Literature*. New York, 1968.
LESTER, Dee Gee, *Irish Research: A Guide to Collections in North America, Ireland and Great Britain*. Westport, Conn., 1987.
Library of Congress, *John Fitzgerald Kennedy: A Chronological List of References*. Washington 1964.
NEWCOMB, Joan, *John F. Kennedy: An Annotated Bibliography*. Metuchen, N.J., 1977.
RACHLIN, Harvey. *The Kennedys: A Chronological History, 1823–Present*. New York, 1986.
RYAN, Dorothy and Louis J., *The Kennedy Family of Massachusetts: A Bibliography*. Westport, Conn., 1981.
SABLE, Martin H., *A Bibliography of the Kennedy Family*. Scarecrow Press, 1969.

VI. Newspapers

Belfast Telegraph. June 1963
Boston Globe, July 1960
Connacht Tribune, June 1963
Cork Examiner, June 1963
Irish Independent. July 1938, June, October–November 1963
Irish Press, July 1938, June 1963
Irish Times, June–July 1963, March 1993
New Röss Echo, June, Aug. 1993
New York Times, July 1938, January 1981
New York Journal American, February 1941, June 1945
Washington Post, June, October 1963

VII. Articles

BARTLETT, Charles, Kenneth W. Thompson, ed., *The Kennedy Presidency*.
BEHAN, Dominic, 'Hail to the O'Chief', *Life*, 5 July 1963.
CARLETON, William G., 'Kennedy in History: An Early Appraisal'. Antioch Review, xxvii (Fall 1964) pp 277–99.
COGLEY, John, 'Kennedy the Catholic', *Commonweal*, 10 Jan. 1964.
Ibid., 'JFK — A Final Word', *Commonweal*, 8 May 1964.
COOGAN, Tim Pat, 'Its County Kennedy Now!', *Irish Digest*, September 1963.
D'ARCY, Frank, 'The Man Whom We Welcome', *Irish Independent*, 26 June 1963.
DOWNEY, James, 'Kennedy and the Years of False Promise', *Irish Times*, 8 November 1980.
EDWARDS, Owen Dudley, articles on Kennedy visit, *Irish Times*, 24–26 June 1963.
Ibid., 'Conclusion: Some Counterthemes', in D.N. Doyle and O.D. Edwards, eds., *America and Ireland, 1776–1976*. Westport, Conn., 1980.
HUTHMACHER, J. Joseph, 'Urban Liberalism and the Age of Reform', *Mississipi Valley Historical Review*, xlix (Sept. 1962) 231–41.
INGLIS, Brian, 'Kennedy in Ireland', *Spectator*, 5 July 1963.
KEMPTON, Murray, 'Looking Back on the Anniversary', *Spectator*, 4 December 1964.
KENNEDY, John F., 'Irish Bases Vital to Britain', *New York Journal American*, 2 February 1941.

Ibid., 'DeValera Aims to Unite Ireland', *New York Journal American*, 29 July 1945.

Ibid., book review — *New York Times Book Review*, September 1959

MITCHELL, Arthur, 'Seeks to Correct "War Party" Label', letter, *Boston Globe*, 6 November 1960.

MUGGERIDGE, Malcolm, 'The Apotheosis of John F. Kennedy', *New York Review of Books*, 28 January 1965.

NOONAN, Arthur, article, *Irish Independent*, 25 November 1963.

O'DONOVAN, Patrick, 'John Kennedy in Europe: Ireland' *Observer*, 30 June 1963.

O'NEILL, Thomas P., articles — *Irish Times*, 24–26 June 1963.

PAYNE, Basil, 'Ireland Today; Image and Reality; Some Reflections on President Kennedy's Visit', *Capuchin Annual, 1964*. Dublin, pp 300–05.

SHANNON, William V., 'J.F.K. in Retrospect', *New York Times*, 19 October 1971.

WALKER, Gerald and Allan, Donald A., 'Jack Kennedy at Harvard', *Coronet*, May 1961.

'Week by Week' column, 'Reality and the American Dream', *Commonweal*, 8 July 1960. Commentary on Archibold MacLeish's statements about Irish Catholics in American society.

VIII. Books

ANON., *A Memory of John F. Kennedy's Visit to Ireland; 26–29 June 1963*. A booklet about the visit.

ANON., *John F. Kennedy; Irish Visit.; Text of Addresses*. Dublin, 1963

BAILEY, Thomas A., *Presidential Greatness*. New York, 1967.

BEATTY, Jack, *The Racal King: The Life and Times of James Michael Curley (1874–1958)*. Reading, Mass., 1992. Interesting on Curley-Kennedy family relationship.

BERNSTEIN, Irving, *Promises Kept: John F. Kennedy's New Frontier*. New York, 1991. At last, a new book extolling the achievements of Kennedy and his Administration.

BESCHLOSS, Michael R., *Kennedy and Roosevelt: The Uneasy Alliance*. London, 1980. A most interesting book; contains short treatment of Joe's 1938 visit to Ireland.

BEW, Paul and Patterson, Henry, *Sean Lemass and the Making of Modern Ireland, 1945–1966*. Dublin, 1982. The story of Ireland's 'Mr. Economic Development'.

BLAIR, Joan and Clay jr., *The Search for JFK*. New York, 1976. The first biography to do a lot of hard digging.

BLANSHARD, Paul, *The Irish and Catholic Power*. Boston, 1953. An alarmist diatribe, but fun to read.

BRADLEE, Benjamin, *Conversations with Kennedy*. New York, 1975. Recollections of journalist friend.

BRAUER, Carl M., *Kennedy and the Second Reconstruction*. New York 1977.

BROWN, Thomas, *JFK: History of an Image*. Bloomington, Indiana, 1988. Comments on books and articles about JFK.

BROWNELL, Blaine A. and Stickle, Warren E., eds., *Bosses and Reformers*. Boston 1973.

BUENKER, John D., *Urban Liberalism and Progressive Reform*. New York, 1973. How the Irish big-city bosses cooperated with middle class Progressives to secure social and economic legislation, 1900–1920.

BURNER, David and West, Thomas R., eds., *The Torch is Passed: The Kennedy Brothers and American Liberalism*. New York, 1964.

BURNS, James M., *John F. Kennedy: A Political Portrait*. 1959 The first biography; balanced but sympathetic.

Ibid., *Edward Kennedy and the Camelot Legacy*. New York, 1975.

COGLEY, John, *Catholic America*. New York, 1973.

COLLIER, Peter and Horowitz, David, *The Kennedys: An American Drama*. New York, 1984. Good reading on a 'popular' level.

COOGAN, Tim Pat., *Ireland Since the Rising*. New York, 1968.

CURLEY, James M., *I'd Do It Again: A Record of all My Uproarious Years*. Englewood Cliffs, N.J., 1957. James Michael's own story.

CUTLER, John H., *Honey Fitz: Three Steps to the White House*. Indianapolis, 1962. Uncritical narrative about an irrepressible man.

DAVIS, John H., *The Kennedys: Dynasty and Disaster, 1848–1983*. 'Popular' treatment by a cousin of Jackie's.

DICKERSON, Nancy, *Among Those Present: A Reporter's View of Twenty-five Years in Washington*. New York, 1976. Nancy, not Angie, has a couple of interesting things to say about Kennedy's sense of Irishness.

DINEEN, Joseph, *The Kennedy Family*. Boston, 1959. Short account by a veteran Boston journalist; some Curley lore.

DOYLE, David N., and O.D.Edwards, eds., *America and Ireland , 1776–1976: The American Identity and the Irish Connection*. Westport, Conn., 1980

DUNCLIFF, William J., *The Life and Times of Joseph P. Kennedy*. New York, 1965. A slight work, with a few original bits.

EDELMAN, Murray, *The Symbolic Uses of Politics*. Urbana, Illinois. 1964.

ERIE, Steven P., *Rainbow's End: Irish-Americans and the Dilemmas of Urban Machine Politics, 1840–1985*. Berkeley, California, 1988. Great scope and scholarly; by far the best book on the subject.

FANNING, Ronan, *Independent Ireland*. Dublin, 1980.

FAY, Paul B, *The Pleasure of His Company*. New York, 1966. Good times with Jack — from the South Pacific to the White House.

FALLOWS, Marjorie, *Irish-Americans: Identity and Assimilation*. New York 1979. Scholarly but readable exposition of the achievements of this group.

FUCHS, Laurence, *John F. Kennedy and American Catholicism*. New York 1967. Jack and his inherited church.

GALLAGHER, Mary Barelli, *My Life With Jacqueline Kennedy*. New York, 1969.

GIGLIO, James M., *The Presidency of John F. Kennedy*. Lawrence, Kansas, 1991.

GLAZER, Nathan and Moynihan, Daniel, *Beyond the Melting Pot: The Negroes, Puerto Ricans, Jews, Italians and Irish of New York City*. Cambridge, Mass., 1963.

GLEASON, Philip, *Keeping the Faith: American Catholicism, Past and Present*. Notre Dame, Indiana, 1987. Includes some on that one among fifty million.

GOODWIN, Doris Kearns, *The Fitzgeralds and the Kennedys*. New York 1987. A huge work by a resourceful writer; all you ever wanted to know. . . .

GREELEY, Andrew, *The Irish Americans: The Rise to Money and Power*. New York, 1981.

Ibid., and William C. McCready, *Ethnicity in the United States*. New York, 1974.

HACHEY, Thomas, with Hernon, Joseph and McCaffrey, Lawrence J., *The Irish Experience*. Englewoods, N.J., 1989.

HACKER, Andrew, ed. *Statistical Portrait of the American People*. New York, 1983.

HAMILTON, Nigel, *JFK: Reckless Youth*. New York, 1992. Flashy title to a well-researched book, slightly marred by touches of English social snobbery.

HENNESSY, Maurice, *I'll Come Back in the Springtime: JFK and the Irish*. New York, 1966. Short narrative with the Kennedy speeches.

HERNON, Joseph, with Hachey, T., and McCaffrey, L., *The Irish Experience*.

HERSH, Burton, *The Education of Edward Kennedy: A Family Biography*. New York, 1972. Loaded with information and insight, but somewhat overwritten, occasional preoccupation with smells, decay, etc. (see pp 48–49).

HERZOG, Arthur, *McCarthy for President*. New York, 1969. Clean Gene makes a point — and changes history.

HILSMAN, Roger, *To Move A Nation*. Garden City, N.Y., 1967. What went wrong with Vietnam, by one who helped to wind the clock.

KELLEY, Kitty, *Jackie Oh!*. Secacus, New Jersey, 1978.

KEMPTON, Murray, *America Comes of Middle Age: Columns, 1950–1962*. Boston 1962. Negative commentary on Kennedy.

KENNEDY, Edward M., ed., *The Fruitful Bough*. NewYork, 1965. Heaps of praise for Joe Kennedy and no mention of the Fitzgeralds.

KENNEDY, John F., *Why England Slept*. NewYork, 1940. College senior history thesis with professional rewrite; dull reading.

Ibid., *A Nation of Immigrants*. New York, 1964, orig. 1958. Positive stuff about all the groups 'that made America great'.

KENNEDY, Rose, *Times to Remember: An Autobiography*. London, 1975. As always, Rose remembers the good things.

KOSKOFF, David, *Joseph P. Kennedy: A Life and Times*. Englewood Cliffs, N.J., 1974. Good supplement to Whalen biography .

LATHAM, Earl, ed., *J.F. Kennedy and Presidential Power*. Lexington, Mass., 1972.

LEE, Joseph J., *Ireland, 1912–1985: Politics and Society*. London, 1989.

LEVINE, Edward M., *The Irish and Irish Politicians*. South Bend, Indiana 1966. Centers on Chicago.

LEVY, Mark R. and Kramer, Michael S., *The Ethnic Factor: How America's Minorities Decide Elections*. New York 1973.

LIEBERSON, Gordon, ed., *JFK: As We Remember Him*. London, 1965.

LINCOLN, Evelyn, *My Twelve Years with John F. Kennedy*. New York, 1965. A few interesting vignettes.

LONGFORD, Lord (Frank Pakenham), *Kennedy*. London, 1976.

LONGFORD, Lord and O'Neill, Thomas P., *Eamon de Valera*. Boston, 1971.

LORD, Donald C., *John F. Kennedy: The Politics of Confrontation and Conciliation*. Woodbury, N.Y., 1977. A positive assessment.

LYONS, F.S.L., *Ireland Since the Famine*. London, 1971.

MANCHESTER, William, *Portrait of a President*. New York, 1962. Gush from a sycophantic writer.

Ibid., *One Brief Shining Moment: Remembering Kennedy*. Thorndike, Maine, 1983. Some interesting recollections of personal conversations with Kennedy.

MARTIN, Ralph G., *A Hero for Our Times: An Intimate Story of the Kennedy Years*. New York, 1983. Lots of personal stuff.

McCAFFREY, Lawrence J., *Textures of Irish America*. Syracuse, 1992. Excellent analysis of various aspects of Irish involvement in American life.

Ibid., *The Irish Diaspora in America*. Washington, D.C., 1976.

Ibid., with Hachey, T. and Hernon, J., *The Irish Experience*

McCARTHY, Abigail, *Private Faces; Public Places*. Garden City, New York, 1972.

McCARTHY, Joe, *The Remarkable Kennedys*, New York, 1960. Good happy blather about the special family.

McTAGGART, Lynne, *Kathleen Kennedy: Her Life and Times*. Garden City, N.Y., 1983. Light, gossipy.

MENENDEZ, Albert J., *John F. Kennedy; Catholic and Humanist*. Buffalo, N.Y., 1980.

MURPHY, John A., *Ireland in the Twentieth Century*. Dublin 1975.

NUNNERLY, David., *John F. Kennedy and Britain*. London 1971.

O'BRIEN, Laurence, *No Final Victories*. Garden City, N.Y., 1974. Recollections of a member of the 'Irish Mafia'.

O'DONNELL, Kenneth and Powers, David (with Joe McCarthy), *'Johnny, We Hardly Knew Ye'; Memories of John Fitzgerald Kennedy*. Boston, 1972. A fine political memoir.

O'NEILL, Terence, *The Autobiography of Terence O'Neill*. London, 1972. Odd, slight memoir, which includes a convoluted explanation of how his family appropriated the great Ulster name of O'Neill.

O'NEILL, Thomas P. and Longford, Lord, *Eamon de Valera*. Boston, 1971.

O'NEILL, Thomas P. 'Tip'. *Man of the House: The Life and Political Memoirs of Speaker Tip O'Neill*. New York 1987. Tip has some revealing things to say about the Massachusetts beginnings; he could have said twice as much — about everthing.

PARMET, Herbert, *JFK: The Presidency of John Fitzgerald Kennedy*. New York, 1983.

Ibid, Jack: *The Struggles of John F. Kennedy*. New York, 1990. Lots of new information.

REAGAN, Ronald, *An American Life*. New York, 1990. A few lines about Ronnie's Irish-American father and Reagan's presidential visit to Ballyporeen, Co. Tipperary. Strongly recommended — for insomniacs.

REEVES, Thomas C., *A Question of Character: A Life of John F. Kennedy*. New York, 1971. Rev. Mr. Reeves sits in judgement.

RUSSELL, Francis, *The Great Interlude*, New York, 1964. Includes an article, 'John the Bold: Boston's John F. "Honey Fitz" Fitzgerald'

SALINGER, Pierre, *With Kennedy*. Solid memoir of Kennedy press secretary.

SARBAUGH, Timoth J., 'John F. Kennedy, the Catholic Issue and Presidential Politics, 1959–1960', Ph.D. dissertation, Loyola University of Chicago, 1987.

SCHLESINGER, Arthur M., jr., *A Thousand Days*. New York, 1965. Account of the Kennedy presidency by the house historian.

Ibid., *Robert Kennedy and His Times*. Boston, 1978. Some interesting additional comments on the clan.

SCHWAB, Peter and Shneidman, J. Lee, *John F. Kennedy*. New York, 1974. Claims the Ks suffered grave social disabilities because of Irish Catholic background.

SEARLS, Hank, *The Lost Prince: Young Joe, the Forgotten Kennedy*. New York, 1969. Well researched and fair-minded.

SHANNON, William V., *The American Irish*. New York, 1963. Essential background reading.

SIDEY, Hugh, *John F. Kennedy: Portrait of a President*. New York 1964. The best biography written while Kennedy was president, but contains nothing concerning the 'Irish connection'.

SORENSON, Theodore, *Kennedy*. New York, 1965. A good narrative by the principal Kennedy speech writer.

THOMPSON, Laurane and Winnick, R.H., *Robert Frost: The Later Years, 1938–1963*. New York, 1976. A couple of interesting things about the old poet and the young president.

THOMPSON, Kenneth W., ed., *The Kennedy Presidency*. New York, 1985. Excellent interviews with Kennedy's people.

TOBIN, Fergal, *The Best of Decades: Ireland in the 1960s*. Dublin, 1984.

WALSH, James B., ed., *The Irish: America's Political Class*. New York, 1976. A couple of articles dealing with Kennedy, including William G. Carleton, 'Kennedy in History: an Early Appraisal'.

WHALEN, Richard, *The Founding Father: The Story of Joseph P. Kennedy*. New York, 1964. Revealing study of old Joe.

WHITE, Theodore H., *The Making of the President: 1960*. New York, 1961.
Lively story of 1960 election, with the winner in the spotlight.

Ibid., *Making of the President: 1964*. New York, 1965. Good account
of Kennedy's anticipation of this election.

Ibid., *In Search of History: A Personal Adventure*. New York, 1978.
Brief recollection of his times with Jack.

WILLS, Garry, *The Kennedy Imprisonment: A Meditation on Power*.
Boston, 1982. A bitterly negative examination of a politically
ambitious family.